The Accidental Insurance Agent

How one day changed my life

Published by Lynn O. High

First Edition 2017

ISBN: 978-1544139609

Preface

This is my story of how I became one of the top salesman in the life insurance industry "by accident" upon being motivated by a severe career altering event.

This event occurred on October 31, 1986, one month before the end of my twenty-year military career. It was a severe personal setback for me – one I pray never happens to you.

As a result of this event my second career following military service was not my dream job. Instead I began a twenty-seven year career selling life insurance earning national "Agent of the Year" four times.

I also helped build a very successful specialty insurance agency and consulting firm.

This is my life story of triumph, then defeat, followed by yet another triumph.

My story offers anyone in sales real life examples of do's and don'ts through recounting actual personal sales events and the lessons learned from them.

These lessons that apply to anyone who desires to succeed in the dog eat dog world of high-end sales.

Table of Contents

Introduction

On Friday, October 31st, 1986, at 1:00 pm PST my world collapsed.

I was living in Las Vegas, Nevada, and at that moment ardently listening to the radio with great anticipation.

Richard Armitage, Assistant Secretary of Defense for International Security Affairs, was holding a live press conference in Washington, D.C., to announce the winner of a fly-off between the General Dynamics F-16N and the Northrop F-20.

The winner would become the follow-on foreign military sales fighter aircraft.

One month before I had declined promotion to the rank of colonel and applied for retirement from the U.S. Air Force.

I was assured by my former air force boss, now a vice president with Northrop that the F-20 was a "shoe-in" to win.

Selection of the Northrop F-20 meant I would become a world-wide sales representative for that aircraft – my dream job.

"Hush," I told my wife as the press conference began.

"Ladies and gentleman," Mr. Armitage began. "The Department of Defense has selected the, (pause), the General Dynamics F-16N as the follow-on foreign military sales fighter aircraft."

My heart stopped. I was in shock. I couldn't speak or think.

My wife said, "What does that mean?"

I didn't hear her. She touched my shoulder and repeated, "What does that mean?"

"It means I am unemployed and we will not be moving to California," I chokingly replied.

We sat and stared at each other in total silence.

In about an hour the phone rang and it was my former boss telling me that he was more than stunned – he was devastated.

He said his wife was crying and he most likely would soon be unemployed (and that came true for him in ninety days).

He added he was sorry for misleading me and wondered what I would do now.

"I have no idea," I replied.

He was my friend and mentor; and now, as he continued to talk with me, he was searching for some kind words to share with me, like when you find yourself at a funeral and are trying to console a grieving widow.

Devastation knows no bounds and finds no friends.

> "I hadn't thought out the obvious fears about money and my future; that losing my job would make me feel inadequate and a bit useless. That it would be harder to get up in the morning when I was shocked into consciousness by the alarm. That I might miss the people I once worked with."
> - Abridged from "Me Before You" by Jojo Moyes

But I didn't let this stop me. No, I picked myself back up and decided I had to find a new future. And by accident I did.

Part 1: Tax shelter selling

Five years before the fateful radio announcement on October 31, 1986, that changed my life, I was transferred from Nellis AFB, Las Vegas, Nevada, to Hickam AFB, Honolulu, Hawaii, arriving on September 5, 1981.

I had just been promoted to lieutenant colonel and had been selected for the Pacific Air Force Inspector General team as an operations and safety inspector.

Before I left Las Vegas for Hawaii I was given the name of a real estate agent to contact and help me find a house. Her name was Marian Cochran.

She was a close friend of an escrow agent I had used to purchase eight rental houses in Las Vegas. I had sold my personal residence before I left for Hawaii and had ready cash to find a place in Honolulu.

I called Marian several weeks in advance of my departure and she had sent me several listings that I found to be favorable. I discussed renting an apartment but she shied me away from that as housing prices in Honolulu were on an upward vector and she convinced me that owning was best.

On arrival in Hawaii I stayed on base for several days and during that time Marian showed me a dozen places. I made offers on two and both came through as they were assumptions of existing mortgages with down payments of under $5,000 each.

One was a condominium on the north side of Pearl Harbor that I bought outright as a rental and Marian had it occupied the day after closing.

The other was a nice little three bedroom house on stilts about nine miles west of Pearl Harbor in a very quiet area near Barbers Point Naval Air Station. I liked it a lot and was going to move in after I returned from my first trip with the inspector general team, which occurred five days after I arrived in Hawaii.

When I returned at the end of September, I had a message at my office from Marian asking me to delay moving in until I could meet with her. I called her immediately and she told me she had a better opportunity for me and asked me to meet her the next morning at 469 Ina Rd – right in the heart of Waikiki.

I arrived and found a place to park (which was always a challenge in Honolulu) and then walked up to a very tall condominium building called the Waipuna. Marian was waiting in the lobby and together we headed to the elevators.

Once in an elevator, I noticed the floor buttons went to 38 and Marian pushed number 37. When the doors opened on the 37th floor she walked slightly to the left, unlocked a tall door and ushered me into the unit ahead of her.

Wow. What a spectacular sight. There was a carved rosewood dining table and chairs with a crystal chandelier to my left, a small kitchen to my right, and right in front of me was a large living room with crystal sconces for light fixtures, a long carved rosewood TV cabinet, a triple plush velvet sofa with two matching overstuffed velvet chairs, and two exquisite alabaster lamps on carved rosewood end tables. It was impressive.

I walked out onto the lanai (balcony for mainlanders) and the view spanned out across Waikiki Beach from Diamond Head to Sand Island. Looking downward, virtually beneath my feet, lay the Hilton Hawaiian Village hotel complex.

After a moment to catch my breath, Marian began her sales pitch.

4

Her husband's father owned the condo but they had to place him in a nursing home in California several months before. They didn't want to rent this incredible property to anyone they did not know and trust.

She had told her husband about me and together, she said, they felt I would be a perfect tenant. I would be gone over half of each month and was clearly not the kind of person that would mistreat the property.

Of course I was flattered at what she said and I had clearly fallen in love with the place, but I had to tell her that I doubted I could afford the rent.

She replied that it would easily rent for $3,000 a month but they would let me have it for half of that amount.

My only utility would be electric, and since there was no heat or air conditioning in nearly every high-rise in Honolulu at that time, she said the bill had never been over a hundred a month.

Further, she went on, I would really like the night life of Waikiki much better than the peace and quiet of Barbers Point. I could walk everywhere along the beach from here, and being in a restricted entry high-rise I would not have to worry about burglaries which were rampant in Hawaii.

Finally, the place came with two parking spaces and parking was a premium in Waikiki.

I turned to her and said, "Looks like I'm going to have another rental property. Will you handle that for me?"

With a smile she replied, "I'll manage both of your properties at no charge so long as I get to sell them when you leave."

I quickly agreed, and with that I was now going to live in a 2,100 square foot three bedroom penthouse 370 feet in the air.

I loved it.

Living at the top
of the world on
Waikiki beach

After setting me on the path of becoming a Waikiki resident living in a posh penthouse, I knew it was the start of a beautiful friendship between Marian and me.

"People don't ask for facts in making up their minds. They would rather have one good, soul-satisfying emotion than a dozen facts."

- Robert Keith Leavit

Chapter 1
You'll never be paid what you're really worth!

In late October I returned from my second inspection trip to our Pacific bases and found a message in my post box at the Waipuna. It was from Marian Cochran, my realtor and now landlady. The note asked me to call her as soon as possible.

Thinking something was amiss, I called as soon as I got to the 37th floor (remember this is way before cell phones).

She answered right away and thanked me for calling saying she wanted to know if I was free that night.

Marian invites me to a seminar

When I first met Marian, I had mentioned that I was an investor in the stock market as well as real estate. It turned out that she was more than a realtor; she was also a Series 22 registered representative for limited partnership security sales.

With a little reluctance I listened to her pitch about a seminar being given by a local securities firm at a hotel not far from my penthouse. There would be free Hawaiian food and a cash bar after the presentation.

I thought to myself, "Why not," and agreed to meet her there at 6:15pm.

The presentation was sponsored by the E.A Buck Company and the primary speaker was Mr. Ed Buck, founder and owner.

To my surprise, Mr. Buck was my age and gave a very convincing presentation on buying limited partnership shares in a commodities trading fund.

After the presentation, Marian introduced me to him and told him about me. He took a keen interest in my being in the military.

He shared he had been a school teacher for many years until he discovered Amway. He became so successful with Amway that he left teaching to live in Japan for three years selling Amway products and recruiting sales representatives under him.

Ed moved on to visit with other guests, so Marian filled me in on a lot more. His success in Japan had made him a millionaire. He was now building a sales force by offering people training to obtain a Series 22/63 license and then act as finders for his company.

If a finder brought a potential client (that being me in this example) and the client bought any offering, the finder (that being Marian) would receive a 2% commission. Finders had to work with a company sales representative who was over them, and that representative also received a 2% commission.

This intrigued me so Marian asked me to another seminar where Mr. Buck was recruiting people to be finders. He gave a convincing presentation that ended with his drawing a mountain on a flip chart with a bunch of dollar signs at the top.

Then Ed said the following, "If you ever want to be paid what you are truly worth, you must be on commission. Only then can your talents and skills be rewarded for what you do."

I was stunned. I had never heard that before.

Ed continued, "If you are on salary, the company paying you has to earn far more from your efforts in order to cover your cost and all of the company's overhead in order to make a profit."

Again, I was dumbstruck. How true.

As a military officer on a fixed paycheck the only way to earn more was through promotions and they had long time intervals. As a result, I was always less than pleased with my income.

I had watched many of my early air force pilot friends leave the military to be airline pilots and they all earned more than I did.

Other friends and relatives my age who never went into the military were professionals or sales reps or business owners and they all made a lot more than I did.

I walked away from that presentation feeling cheated; cheated by the air force for holding me back financially.

Becoming a registered representative

The very next day I went to the E.A. Buck office and signed up for the Series 22/63 class. I had to pay a fee to cover all of the books and the two license exams, as well as cover the instructor, but I jumped on it.

I then met with the senior manager of the school and worked out a schedule for classes as I was always away each month for 16-20 days on my inspection trips. He agreed to work with me saying they had constant training classes at different stages and I could come and go as needed. All I had to do was pass the SEC exams.

I received my study books and they were huge. Besides general information, they contained thousands of questions in the format of the SEC exams. If you studied them diligently, you would have an answer bank in your head. Being a pilot I had a head for memorizing many things required to fly, so I felt I could do this.

I returned in November and did a week of double classes. I passed the practice exams over and over and my instructor agreed to register me for the two SEC exams in the first week of January, 1982. I studied more on my December trip and over Christmas break and took the exams in January before my next trip.

When I returned the end of January, I learned that I had passed both exams with flying colors.

NOTE: A Series 22 registration allows one to sell limited partnerships that directly own things, like apartment complexes, oil wells, cable TV systems, public storage facilities, and commodities; anything that could be packaged into a partnership. The Series 63 is the regulatory license required of every one. In addition, a registered representative had to obtain a state registration under the Series 63 for each state in which one wanted to sell.

And then the hard part set in. The Buck organization had more training – training on products and how to make cold calls.

Oops! Cold calls? The only thing close to a cold call I had ever made was calling a girl in high school or college for a date. And I thought making those calls was as close as possible to hell on earth.

Chapter 2
Introduction to cold calling

The E.A. Buck Company (Buck) had two training tracks you had to complete before they allowed anyone to solicit a prospect to attend one of their seminars.

The first track was to study the products they sold and then pass an internal written exam and a verbal exam. That was the easy part for me. No problem for my steel trap mind.

For the second track, I had to study sales call scripts and then role play these scripts with a company training officer. That was my first ever role play and I thought it was sheer hell.

Then, after several sessions of role playing cold calls, I had to begin to call real people. Now the proverbial crap hit the fan.

Here I was, a highly decorated veteran of two combat tours, but calling a total stranger with a pitch to come to an investment seminar was more frightening than all of the thousands of anti-aircraft guns, surface to air missiles, and enemy fighters that had shot at me over 440 combat missions.

I was terrified – terrified of this little device and the person on the other end.

Hell on earth

I stuttered, I stammered, I felt like an ass for invading these people's privacy. But I had to do this.

My trainer reiterated that the only way to reach the top of the mountain and earn the money was to do this. You had to have clients attend seminars and then buy a product to earn a commission. It was a simple as that.

Buck had dozens of lists of doctors and other people of high net worth for us to call. Back in the '80's privacy and unlisted phone numbers were not a big deal. You could buy lists of thousands of people's phone numbers and Buck did that.

After several months of trying cold calls and not getting anyone to attend a seminar, I was ready to quit. And then it struck me.

A new idea

I had a wealthy sister who was a doctor and my father was retired and of considerable net worth. Maybe I should approach them?

I called my sister first, as I knew that she had high income, and told her all about what I was doing. She quickly said she always wanted tax shelters and was looking for one at that time.

You see, in the 1981 tax reform passed under President Reagan, her top tax bracket was now 50% and she had a 5% state tax rate on top of that. Any tax write-offs were serious options for her.

All of our big offerings were exempt from public registration under Reg D for qualified investors. They were in units of $50,000 and all took cash or recourse loans.

I quickly registered in her state, and during my visit on leave back on the mainland in July, she bought an apartment offering from me. I had made my first sale to my sister and that 2% commission ($1,000) was the nicest paycheck I had ever received.

When I returned to Hawaii in August, I approached Ed and told him I wanted to be a direct salesman from that point forward and only sell the big offerings.

He balked at first, but Marian, who was my up-link and had received her first check for $1,000 on my sister's deal, interceded saying she was happy to release me, so Ed agreed.

In the fall my father, who had unearned income and was in the 70% bracket, and my sister each bought one unit for $50,000 of an oil drilling venture. Since I was now my own sales representative, I made 4% ($2,000) on each sale. "Wow," I thought, "this is nice."

I had now made a total of $150,000 in sales and Ed was very proud of me. Most of the standard offerings of public partnerships were for units of $2,000 per sale; not $50,000. I had made it to the big time in his operation.

Life in an alternative world

Ed taught me a lot about sales during the next ten months before I left Hawaii in July, 1983. He taught me to not give up, to study to be very knowledgeable about taxes and investments, and most of all to treat potential clients with respect and never burn a bridge. Good advice for a "green" registered representative.

But I still hated making cold calls and became determined to find a better way to engage prospects.

NOTE: I had to obtain approval from the air force to hold these licenses and was restricted to only sell on non-duty days or when on leave. I could not have a conflict of

13

interest with my work, and could not sell to anyone in the armed forces junior to me in rank. I honored these rules at all times.

Before I left Hawaii to attend the Air War College, I had two ideas hit me.

The first idea was to write a book about everything I had learned in Hawaii; and the second idea was to develop a better way to find prospects.

"Obstacles are necessary for success because in selling, as in all careers of importance, victory comes only after many struggles and countless defeats."

- Og Mandino

Chapter 3
Seminars for riches

Becoming a satellite securities office

I left Hawaii on July 8, 1983, to attend the Air War College located in Montgomery, Alabama in August. This is a very prestigious military school as only about 10% of all colonels are selected to attend; and I was one of them.

But…before I left Hawaii I discussed with Ed how I could remain a detached representative of his company.

I had made three more oil drilling venture sales during the spring of 1983, one to myself, one more to my sister and one more to my father, so I had another $150,000 in sales under my belt.

Although he had in-house sales representatives that did far more than I, they were full time and I was part-time. I would always be ranked against over 200 finders and dual status finder/salesmen.

It turns out at that point in time, I was Ed's leading part-time sales representative and he was totally open to finding a way for me to stay engaged with his firm.

Ed and I met with his registration and compliance staff and they said it was possible to make me a "satellite" office of the company.

I would have to take two new SEC exams to do so, and then maintain files of all of my prospect calls, copies of all correspondence to anyone, use only company approved literature, and records of whatever I sold.

I would have to provide the same documentation to the central office in Honolulu, as both of us could be inspected by the SEC.

I agreed and they agreed and after doing more paperwork to become registered with the SEC I went on to Alabama.

Buck set up the two exams for me at the nearest location in Birmingham, Alabama. On the day I was scheduled for the exams I took a day of leave and drove to Birmingham.

I passed them both and became a junior office of jurisdiction of the E. A. Buck Company. This allowed me to sell directly in any state in which I was registered.

But as I said at the end of the previous chapter, I still hated making cold calls and needed to find a better way to obtain prospects.

No more cold calling

I put my thinking cap on and analyzed my best strengths and quickly found two.

First, I loved to sell at the client level. If I could see the client I knew I could make the sale.

Second, I was a master at making presentations. During a prior staff tour at Tactical Air Command in Langley, Virginia, in 1976-78, I had made dozens of presentations to generals and several to foreign delegations.

I had also attended the Armed Forces Staff College in Norfolk, Virginia, in the first half of 1979 where I further honed my presentation and public speaking skills. And during my just completed tour with the Inspector General team I had become the head of the presentation team for the final out briefing to the commander and his staff of the unit we had just inspected.

I could stand up and present anything to anyone. I possessed two of the three most important skill sets for selling.

I decided on seminar selling like Ed did in Hawaii and created a 35mm slide show all about the E.A. Buck Company and its products.

I then approached my sister and asked her to host a group of her doctor friends for me to make a presentation to them. She told them that they were under no obligation to work with me, but only listen to my ideas and make their own decisions.

I began with a seminar for fifteen doctors on Monday, November 21, 1983. That was the beginning of the Thanksgiving holiday week and the war college was closed for the entire week.

On that Monday evening I struck more money than all the oil wells I had sold combined. My presentation was a hit.

In preparation I had read a book about selling to doctors. It is very true that a surgeon thinks and makes decisions very differently than a pediatrician. My sister helped too, outlining the various personality types of her doctor friends.

Long and short selling tax shelters with between 80% of the investment dollars to 200% of the investment dollars as a tax write-off was like selling ice in hell. I closed $350,000 in sales that Thanksgiving. I was in heaven.

I returned again at Easter break and gave another seminar for more doctors and did another $450,000 of sales. By then it was another tax year and many prior clients wanted add-on business.

I continued to sell to these doctors until the 1986 tax reform act passed by President Reagan, which shut down all of these huge tax write-off strategies. In exchange for the loss of deductions, and caps on write-offs, a top tax rate of 39.6% was created.

Many other restrictions were in the 1986 tax reform and still exist to this day. As a result, investing for pure tax avoidance lost its luster; but many of the programs I sold made huge returns.

Lessons learned

From my beginning in sales in 1982 to the end of 1986, I learned the following three principles:

1. Your prospect has to first trust you and believe that you have their best interest at heart. If they don't it's over.

2. Your prospect has to trust your company. Will they deliver on the promises they make through you?

3. Your prospect has to believe in the products you are recommending to them. Are they legitimate and will they pay him back. Would you put your life savings in them?

"The best way to sell yourself to others is first to sell the others to yourself."

- Napoleon Hill

If your client trusts you on all three of these principles, you can keep them forever. Trust is the one commodity that once lost is never regained.

I had one doctor buy only oil wells. I urged him to diversify. I too bought too many oil wells – and we both lost money.

He still trusts me to this day for two reasons.

First, he went against my advice; and second, I lost money right along with him.

For my diversified clients they all made a lot of money and he saw that. For example, cable TV ventures paid the greatest return from 2-5 times the investment in 2-4 years.

In short, success in the sales business comes from having happy clients with whom you never lose trust. Period.

Writing a book

During my ten months at the Air War College I wrote my first book called Pay Yourself First.

Before I left Hawaii, I shipped my car to Los Angeles and then drove it across the USA spending time at stops along the way to visit friends and relatives.

But all along the way I talked into a tape recorder. I unloaded everything I knew about tax shelters, investing strategies, and ideas on gaining wealth from books I had read in Hawaii.

I sent the tapes back to a legal secretary I had met in Hawaii and she transcribed them onto typed pages.

I then re-typed those pages into my brand new Kaypro II computer (picture on next page).

Thank goodness I could type at over 150 words a minute.

After doing the typing, I edited what I had typed and stayed up almost every weeknight until 11 or 12. My new wife, my girlfriend from Honolulu, complained often but those long hours resulted in my first book.

After graduating from the war college, I was transferred back to Nellis AFB, Las Vegas, Nevada. I had been selected to be a part of the leadership team for the Aggressor adversary tactics program. You may recall that I had been assigned there five years earlier as a major after attending the armed forces staff college in 1979.

Almost immediately after I arrived, I went looking for and found a small printing company that would simply print the book for me. They would just use my layouts and print from those pages.

As a result, I totally self-published my book and sold it myself through mail order ads in military magazines. And then one more idea hit me.

Why not use my book as a special giveaway at the large investment seminars that Ed Buck held twice a year in Honolulu.

> "So long as new ideas are created, sales will continue to reach new highs."
>
> - Dorothea Brande

I called Ed and proposed that I come to Honolulu for these special seminars and open the presentations with an outline of the key principles in my book.

Ed didn't have to think twice – he accepted my proposal immediately. You see, for the past two years I had been his top part-time salesman. He liked me and my ideas.

Over the next two years I made four trips to Honolulu and opened his three-hour presentations with a thirty minute outline of my book.

As part of his advertising for these seminars, he offered each attendee a free copy of my book indicating the author would be available to sign the attendees' copy after the presentation. Each seminar had between 350-500 attendees and one had just over 600 people attend. I signed a lot of books.

He also gave my book away at his smaller monthly seminars that he conducted in his office building, and a good number of his sales representatives used it in their presentations too.

In total he bought over 5,000 copies from me. He paid my airfare and hotel to Hawaii for his seminars and my profit was a two dollar markup on the books which cost two dollars to print.

I further sought out three local brokerage offices in Las Vegas and customized my book with their logos and gave a twenty minute presentation at over twenty seminars held by them.

So there you have it. I sold over 9,000 copies of my book by mail order, one at a time, and 9,000 copies to sponsors of investment seminars.

But then, October 31st, 1986, occurred.

"Nothing in the world is worth having or worth doing unless it means effort, pain, difficulty… I have never in my life envied a human being who led an easy life. I have envied a great many people who led difficult lives and led them well."

- Theodore Roosevelt

"The harder you fall, the heavier your heart; the heavier your heart, the stronger you climb; the stronger you climb, the higher your pedestal."

- from "Killosophy" by Criss Jami

Part 2: Personal life insurance selling

<u>Disaster strikes</u>

In the introduction to this book I outlined what happened on Friday, October 31, 1986.

On that date, I was set to retire from the air force in sixty days and planed on moving to California to work for the Northrop Corporation. I was going to sell their new F-20 fighter jet to foreign allies (based on the government's selection of that plane).

Rather, on that Friday, a fateful announcement by the Department of Defense threw a horrible curve into my life as they selected Northrop's competitor, General Dynamics, to provide the future allied low-cost fighter (which actually never happened).

Saturday passed very slowly for me. I was sick in my stomach with worry and my wife had cried most of the night before from fear of what would happen to us. We simply sat at home in shock.

Sunday seemed a little bit better for us both, as the shock and pain had become simple numbness. I went out mid-morning and bought the local Sunday newspaper and began to study the help-wanted ads. I also went to work on a resume.

Turns out my resume read very well for a sales job. In the prior summer, I had taken the Series 7 exam which made me a fully qualified registered representative authorized to sell any security product. And of course I had written my book. I had pulled together what I thought would be a very good resume to commence my search for employment.

On Monday I called my first ad from the Sunday paper. It was with New York Life, but when the lady who answered the phone asked me some questions, like my age and what I had been doing, she quickly said they were only looking for recent college graduates.

I cut her off and literally directed her to tell the hiring officer that I already had a Series 7 license and had written two books on personal finance.

NOTE: I had also written a short book titled "The Ten Commandments of Wealth" in 1985 and sold over 7,000 copies of it to private securities groups.

In a moment the hiring officer was on the phone. After I outlined my background, he quickly asked me to come to an orientation meeting on Wednesday evening; and I quickly agreed.

Next I called a local office of a regional brokerage firm and was quickly offered an interview that afternoon. At the interview, they were so impressed with my already having a Series 7 license and several years of successful sales experience that they offered me an immediate sales position.

I also called one other brokerage office that morning and over the phone they offered me a position.

To understand, these positons were all commissioned sales so their risk was minimal. I sold myself, my prior production numbers, and my licenses to them very well.

But another option occurred along the road in my job search.

Which way do I go?

Fortune comes calling

About a week before October 31st I had called the Lutheran Brotherhood home office in Minneapolis, Minnesota, asking to have a representative call me to discuss my life insurance needs.

I had two old Lutheran Brotherhood whole life policies, one for $1,000 that my father had bought for me when I was six months old, and another for $10,000 that I had bought when I was sixteen. Together they had about $5,000 of cash value.

Shortly after my call to the home office a man from Phoenix, Arizona, called saying that Las Vegas was part of their agency and he would be in town the next week. He was available to meet with me on Monday evening.

We agreed on a 6:00pm appointment and I emphasized to him that he needed to be on time as I had a meeting on base that evening. I explained my military situation so he understood the importance of this request.

Monday, November 3, 1986

Six o'clock came and went. I was already in my uniform and began to be concerned. Finally, at 6:25pm the doorbell rang.

I pulled the door open and two men were standing outside. I literally ordered them to enter and began in a less than kindly manner to inform them that they were late and I had little time before I would need to leave.

I quickly told them my situation and the two policies I already had with their company. I said I needed new coverage as my military insurance would terminate at retirement and my outside military

25

association coverages would nearly double in cost upon retirement. I needed some better options.

They quickly explained universal life to me and asked how much I thought I needed. I replied, "Two hundred thousand."

The agent replied that if I went to $250,000 it would have a lower internal cost of insurance. He further said that I could roll-over my two small policies and use that cash value as a foundation for future cash value growth. The premium could be at whatever amount I wanted.

I told him to write it up – probably the easiest sale he had ever made.

Then the other man spoke. His name was Gregg Knudten and he was twenty-six years old and the assistant general agent for the agency in Phoenix.

He began to ask me what I was going to do after my retirement from the air force and I quickly gave him a Reader's Digest version of the past four days.

His face began to shine and he asked me if he were to stay overnight (they both had flown in that morning and had the last flight back to Phoenix that evening) would I be able to meet with him in the morning.

I queried why and he said they needed a new agent in Las Vegas. Their only one was retiring shortly and if I went with them versus New York Life, I would be their only agent in Clark County.

Then he added that the company had 2,000 orphan policies which could be a fantastic opportunity for me.

I didn't know what that meant, and I had to leave, so I said, "Okay, I will meet you at exactly eight in the morning."

I said I would have a base entry pass waiting for him at the gate when he arrived and the guards would tell him how to get to my office. Then I curtly added that I would have less than an hour to see him and told him not to be late.

"Yes sir," he replied.

I signed the forms put in front of me and left telling them my wife would handle the rest.

Tuesday, November 4, 1986

Every Tuesday began with a meeting at 7:00am with the commanding general of our wing (a one-star).

It was attended by all of the deputy commanders and other colonels who ran things. I was still the official deputy commander for adversary tactics until my replacement graduated from our extensive Aggressor course in two more weeks.

I was scheduled to brief to fly at 9:00am and had arrived on base at 6:30am. I called the main gate to provide clearance for Mr. Knudten to come on base and asked the guard to give him directions to my building.

I walked into my building at about 7:50am and Gregg was sitting in my outer office. I asked him to follow me, and the discussion that followed opened a new window for my life.

> "Don't think that things can't change. Things can change for the better in an instant. Keep believing, keep standing, and keep hoping."
>
> - Tahj Mowry

Opportunity knocks

Gregg began by telling me his agency in Phoenix had been selected as the trial agency for a new sales program called the Lifetime Economic Acceleration Program (LEAP).

It was complex and would require a one-week training course beginning the second week of December. I would not have to learn the old needs analysis system and Gregg thought this new program would drive sales up and away.

After learning about me, my Series 7 and past selling experience, and being the author of two books on personal finance, Gregg was convinced that I would be a natural for his company.

On the spot he offered me the position of sole agent in Clark County Nevada.

I told him I officially went on final leave from the military on December 1st and he could not have arrived at a better time.

He then explained that having 2,000 orphan policies transferred to me as agent of record would be a foundation that could provide me with hundreds of sales.

Orphans are people with an old policy who no longer live where the policy was acquired or no longer do business with their company. Orphans were just "out there."

Since the one and only agent in Las Vegas was retiring, he had never bothered to call on them other than when they called him for service work. All he really did was collect the service fees (a small annual fee is paid to the agent of record on every policy) and find new clients.

But slowly, in that short hour, I realized that I had been saved from my disaster by this chance encounter with Mr. Gregg Knudten.

Lady Luck was with me. I was saved by a roll of the dice with Gregg right then in fabulous Las Vegas.

"Did you ever observe to whom the accidents happen? Chance favors only the prepared mind."

- Louis Pasteur

"I believe that everything happens for a reason. People change so that you can learn to let go, things go wrong so that you appreciate them when they're right, and sometimes good things fall apart so better things can fall together."

- Marilyn Monroe

Chapter 4

When you come to a fork in the road, take it

Yoga Bera said that. He is famous for his twisted about comments like, "It's déjà vu all over again."

For me, his sayings seemed more applicable than ever before during those topsy-turvy days in the fall of 1986.

I began my final retirement leave on Monday, December 1, 1986, with an official date of retirement of January 1, 1987.

Gregg came up to Las Vegas with a stack of paperwork for me to sign to become an agent and registered representative of Lutheran Brotherhood.

He then spent two days going over all kinds of guides for conduct, how the new portable computer illustration system and portable battery driven heat printer worked, and how to set up my office.

I had a third bedroom in my house that I converted into my office. I added a house phone line extension, and installed a new fax and computer line dedicated to my new profession.

I also had to take one exam, the LIMRA sales aptitude evaluation, and I barely passed it. Oh well, perhaps not a harbinger of things to come, but it did startle me a bit.

As I mentioned earlier, the Phoenix agency had been selected as a pilot for a new sales system (LEAP).

The existing sales system was one that simply took data from a prospect and added up all of his and her family obligations and survivorship needs, then compared that total to the family's existing assets and life insurance, and voilà, the end result was how much life insurance the prospect(s) needed.

This prior system was officially called Needs Assessment and had been used for years and years. I was thrilled that I would not be using it.

Learning how to LEAP

The new system being introduced for testing in their agency was the Lifetime Economic Acceleration Process (LEAP) created by Mr. Robert Castiglione.

I went to Phoenix for four days of training on LEAP and fell in love with it. My initial reaction was that it was ingenious and truly a better way than needs assessment.

But the old heads verbally made it clear that they didn't like it, saying it was not a good way to sell life insurance. They thought it was too complex and the prospect would be overwhelmed, etc.

I quickly figured out why they felt that way as to really make LEAP perform one had to be a bit of a mathematical genius.

Fortunately for me, math was literally my hobby and I took to using discount tables and forecasting future values like a fish to water. I had done all of this in college and during my MBA courses. I had also been an off-duty adjunct instructor for night schools on base the past three years and had been teaching math and statistics, including building forecasting models.

All this was well before personal computers were widespread. To solve a problem, I would take a printed discount table, explain it to a prospect, and then do the math right in front of them. I excelled at using this system.

NOTE: If you want to understand the LEAP system just Google it as it is still used by many salesmen today.

After my week in Phoenix, I returned to Las Vegas and Gregg brought me 2,000 Green Cards. Each one was a little 3X5 card with all the data the company had about the orphaned policies.

I then set about putting all of this information into a data base system on my Kaypro II personal computer. I culled out duplicates and multiple addresses and joined family names together.

Then, since none had a phone number on the Green Card (yes the company had everything but their phone number), I set to work and began looking up names in the phone book. At that time Las Vegas was the only city in the USA that issued two phone books a year due to its highly transient work force.

If a person was not in the book, and a good number of them were not, I then called information to find them. I ended up with about 80% of the final valid cards with phone numbers.

Based on combining multiple family members or policyholders and finding a valid phone number, I ended up with 1,200 good leads. I then did two things.

First, I created a form letter to mail to each one; and second, I took a few days off for Christmas and on Saturday, December 28, and Sunday, December 29, I began calling Green Card prospects.

"Begin by always expecting good things to happen."
-Tom Hopkins

Chapter 5
Cold calling; again

To be up front, I had not really done that much cold calling with the Buck organization (I related that to you in chapter 2).

I figured out a way to avoid it as my sister hosted me for numerous seminars with her doctor friends and from them I received referrals and did not have to do cold calls.

I now approached this new requirement for making calls with a methodical strategy of using a script that went as follows:

Ring, ring.

"Hello"

"Hello, this is Lynn High, your Lutheran Brotherhood area representative. May I speak with David Smith?"

"I am his wife. May I ask what this is about?"

"Yes, I am calling on behalf of the home office of Lutheran Brotherhood to give him some information about new developments with the policy he has with us. Is he available?"

"Just a moment," was the most common reply. And of course, if he answered I would do that same statement to him.

Now I already had the date the policy was issued, and everything about it financially, but not his/her birthday. So I would then follow with something like this:

"David, may I call you David?"

I had learned from reading that using a person's first name makes it less formal and asking permission to do so brings the person's guard down.

"Yes," was the reply 99% of the time.

"David, the home office has asked me to contact you about your policy with Lutheran Brotherhood. I think you must have gotten that policy when you were pretty young. Did your parents buy it for you?"

This was very common with these older policies. Most were for a face amount of $1,000 to $2,500 and had cash value between $200 and $800; thus you could tell the age from the cash value (recall I had a policy my father bought when I was six months old).

"Yes, I was xx years old."

"Well, David, the purpose for my call is to meet with you and explain all of the changes that have occurred since you obtained that policy. Would you be available this Tuesday at 3pm or would Thursday at 7pm be better?"

I knew that Las Vegas was a 24-hour town and had two major work shifts: 8-5 and 5-1am. Offering one day and one evening was a subtle way of learning that. And of course several objections could occur, the most common was:

"What is this about again?"

"I understand David. I need to meet with you to explain some options for your policy that may result in a lower premium or a larger amount of benefit. Would next blah or blah work best for you?"

Or he might say, "Well I work days, so an evening would be better."

"May I ask what you do? Where do you work?"

They would always tell me and then I would simply ask, "Is 7o'clock Tuesday or 9o'clock Thursday best for you?"

They would pick one.

If those times didn't work, they would usually offer another day. If so I would say, "Yes, I am open Wednesday but only at 9o'clock; I already have an appointment at 7. Would 9 work alright for you?"

Gregg had me do a good number of practice phone calls with him earlier in December before I made my first call. He had told me to always make it appear that my time was scarce. I should say I was busy on two of the nights even if this was my very first call for that week. Over time I really mastered this calling system.

For January, 1987, I filled my evenings for two a night, including Friday, as many people worked weekend shifts; and I was able to get six appointments every Saturday.

I never asked for Sunday as I went to church, used the afternoon for slack time, and did all of my calls on Sunday evenings from 7-10pm.

Yes, Sunday evenings. Las Vegas was a 24/7 town. I never had a single person object to being called on Sunday. Some would ask me to call them back during the week and then I would ask for a daytime phone number.

My phone calls went great for the first two months although I was terribly bored during most of the daytime hours.

Real Cold Calls

In March, Gregg insisted that I begin to cold call church directories. He had taken me to most of the area churches to meet the pastors and I had about ten directories including my own church which had over 800 family listings.

I had been knocking the ball out of the park for the past two months with Green Card clients and he pushed me to do these cold calls. He wanted me to broaden my sales exposure and try and obtain an equal share of Green Card clients with non-client individuals from the church directories.

I had made a trip to the home office for training in February and was told letters and notes were part of the concept of multiple contacts. They told me the industry standard was making six contacts to obtain a sale.

I began by writing a letter to the prospect saying I was the newly appointed Lutheran Brotherhood representative in Las Vegas and that I would be giving them a call in the next two weeks.

When I got through to them on the phone, I would mention the letter and a few acknowledged receiving it.

> NOTE: I briefly tried letters with the Green Card clients but quickly dropped it as some would say they received my letter and would call me if they needed anything. I realized there is a thing called too much information too soon.

Then two things began to develop on these new cold calls.

First, we had a competitor called Aid Association to Lutherans (AAL). They were a separate Lutheran fraternal company and we directly competed against them. Quite often I would make a call and the church member already worked with AAL. Although I would try to see them, they were just not interested saying they were happy with AAL.

> NOTE: These two organizations merged years later; today the company is called Thrivent Financial.

Second, it became obvious that getting an appointment with someone that did not have a policy with my company met serious resistance – resistance that I had experienced before in Hawaii. I didn't do well with that.

With the Green Card clients I had a ratio of 8 out of 10 calls resulting in an appointment. With non-clients that dropped to 1 out of 10 calls. And the verbal abuse I encountered on many of those calls was a severe blow to my ego.

I had just retired as a deputy commander at the premier air force fighter wing at Nellis AFB where I had three phones on my desk: a red one reserved for the two generals above me; a black one with three punch buttons for each of the three squadron commanders who reported to me; and a regular black phone that my secretary answered.

Now, I was just a voice on a phone interrupting these people's evening. It became obvious that rejection was not going over well with my psyche.

Occasionally, when a cold call prospect bit, it was fun; but most of the time it was not.

I recall one especially abusive respondent that by chance happened to be in front of me the next Sunday in my church's badge line. We wore pre-printed name badges in my church and they were kept in a large rack at the church entrance.

This man was in front of me and I saw his name badge when he picked it up. I quickly grabbed mine and approached him.

"Mr. Jones, my name is Lynn High. I'm really glad to meet you. We spoke on the phone a week ago."

He turned red and stammered, "I'm so sorry. I shouldn't have said those things to you. It wasn't a Christian thing to do."

"Don't worry," I replied. "I get that more than you may think."

I stuck my hand out and he took it and then apologized once more. I wish I could have heard what he told his wife about me. It could have only gone one of two ways.

Seminars again

After discussions with Gregg (he came to see me every other week) I mentioned how successful I had been at seminars, especially with my presentation skills.

He agreed that would be a good idea. I had used my book, Pay Yourself First, in the past as part of the appeal to attend seminars as each attendee would receive a free copy.

I then embarked on creating a presentation and then calling the church directories to invite them to my financial seminar.

This worked and I continued them for several months; however, the continued pressure of cold calls filled with plenty of verbal abuse continued to deflate my ego and affect my temperament.

Chapter 6
How much do you want?

I have always been an easy sell; but only if it is what I want. In other words, when I walk into a department store to buy a shirt, I don't want anything else; I just want to buy a shirt.

If a salesperson tries to pressure me into an add-on sell, I get very defensive and tell them to forget it. I only buy what I want.

Used car salesmen hate me even worse. I never buy the one they want to sell me; I only buy the one I want and from the dealer who gives me the lowest price for the same commodity.

When I walk into a used car dealer (they call it the pre-owned division now) I have the exact car I am looking to buy in mind. I ask all about it, maybe even test drive it, and then I leave.

I then do the same thing at another dealer. Then I go home and do my research to determine each car's value and my top price. Only then do I return to the dealer who has the car I liked the best and tell them I want to consider buying that car.

I tell them right up front that I have another car at another dealer that I am willing to accept, but they get the first chance to sell me their car. But they get only one chance right now.

At the salesperson's desk I ask them to write on a blank piece of paper how much they will sell that car to me right now, in cash, and drive it home that day.

I then tell them I am writing down what I am willing to pay right now on my piece of paper.

NOTE: This only works on cash deals. If you are trying to trade a car you are totally at the mercy of the dealer. I always sell my trade-in myself to get more money and then be able to buy for cash.

If they play, and most of them will, I ask them to turn their paper over and I will do the same. If my price is greater than their price, they just sold the car at their price. If their price is higher than mine, I get up and walk out the door. I stick to my guns on this. If they lose I leave.

Then I go to the other dealer where I have an acceptable car waiting for my offer and do the same. If he wins I have a car; if not I leave once more, having also told him I have an acceptable car at another dealer.

Then I wait a day. If I did like one better than the other, I go back there first on the next day and lower my price by $50-$100. If the salesman is smart, he did the same. They get really mad when they give you the same price I did the day before, if they can even remember it, and I walk once more.

I do this with the other dealer and if no deal, I tell them I am not going to be back. I have actually had them call me later in the day and offer the car for a couple of hundred below my last offer.

This only works with cash sales, but it does work. So how does this apply to a life insurance prospect?

Can your prospect trust you?

If you remember at the end of chapter 3 in lessons learned, I stated the following three principles:

1. Your prospect has to first trust you and believe that you have their best interest at heart. If they don't, it's over.

2. Your prospect has to trust your company. Will your company deliver on the promises that they make through you?

42

3. Your prospect has to believe in the product(s) you are recommending to them. Are they legitimate for his situation?

"All things being equal, people will do business with, and refer business to, those people they know, like, and trust."

- Bob Burg

If your prospect trusts you on all three of these principles, you can close 80% of them. I did. Here's how I achieved that.

Learning to drink coffee

I will never forget my first four house calls, two on Monday and two on Tuesday, January 6-7, 1987.

At the first meeting, I rang the doorbell promptly at 7pm and a man answered. After stating my name he asked me into his home.

It was a modest house, and I followed him into their living room where he introduced me to his wife. He then offered me a seat on a chair opposite a sofa, and as he sat down his wife asked if I would like a cup of coffee.

"No thank you," I replied

She then sat down beside her husband, crossed her arms as he did, and he said, "Well, what do you want?"

I will never forget those words, and the crossed arms, all of which created a sudden chill in the room.

I gave my opening pitch, and over the next twenty minutes won the option of leaving the LEAP data booklet with them and his saying he would call me when he had completed it. I was out the door by 7:30pm.

I drove to an intersection near my next appointment and sat in my car thinking. Wow, coffee. I never drank coffee during my 20 years in the air force or in college before that. I drank lots of iced tea and Pepsi, but never wanted coffee.

Hmmm. My mind was racing. Guess I better be social with my prospects to start my meetings; after all I had invited myself into their homes. I arrived at my 9pm appointment ten minutes early, and literally the same greeting and seating transpired.

This time when asked if I wanted coffee, I replied eagerly that I did. His wife asked how I took it.

I hadn't thought about that. But having watched many of my Swedish cousins take it with cream and sugar I said that.

I made an innocuous comment about the décor to the husband, and in a minute she returned and handed me a cup.

"Thank you," I said, and then took a sip.

I was so startled by the taste it required all of my willpower to keep from spitting it out. She returned and offered me some cookies, which I accepted hoping they would kill the awful taste of the coffee.

I very slowly nursed the coffee as we continued with some small talk, and when they finished their coffees I began my sales pitch.

"Thank you for sharing your time with me tonight, blah, blah, blah."

The proverbial ice was broken and in about ten minutes we were moving to the kitchen table and discussing their financial future.

The next night I tried coffee with only cream for my first appointment; and the second appointment with only sugar. I was at least prepared for the weird tastes of my choices

On Wednesday evening I said I took my coffee black, and that settled it for me. I have continued to drink coffee to this day; but only black.

LEAP-ing for joy

The LEAP system was incredible. It was made for me as I was quick with the math; and I had two other major strengths that I capitalized upon.

First, I would refer to my book, Pay Yourself First, and give a free copy to every prospect I met. I would use it by turning to various passages during my first visit to build my credibility.

Second, I would tell my prospects right up front during this first visit that I would not ask them to buy anything from me. I would only offer them a product if they asked me to do so in reference to a problem they identified at our next meeting.

Why? Because I had no idea what they needed right then nor did I have any idea what they wanted; that was for the next two meetings. Plus, it totally disarmed them from any resistance to listening to what I had to say.

LEAP had a booklet that was left with the prospect to complete at the end of the first meeting. It asked them for all of their financial information on everything they owned and owed. It was extensive and I would spend time explaining those parts to them during the first meeting.

The booklet also had a section for them to fill in on what their personal goals were for their future. Whatever it was, college for children, owning a home, retirement, any and all personal and financial goals.

I would spend quite a bit of time helping them fill in that section during this first meeting. By doing this together, I become a counselor and trusted confidant. Some would start out with resistance, but within five-ten minutes that was gone as we worked together.

You see, up until that moment, 95% of them had never done anything like this. It opened up their eyes and they became excited putting their dreams onto a piece of paper. Many had never done that in all their years of marriage.

I of course lead them, getting them to talk together about these things, and I created a sense of urgency in their minds to fill in the rest of the data for the next meeting.

Finally, at the end of the meeting, I would autograph my book and make a comment to them on the interior page.

It could almost be funny how the book was used. On several occasions one of them would literally grab it from me during this discussion as I used it for reference by turning pages to look at a diagram or quote. They would follow along with great interest.

When they did that, I would become quiet and let them read or talk about the current idea. Soon they returned to the task at hand and some would offer the book back to me.

But at the end, the autographing of the book was almost like a solemn pledge for them to work with me.

NOTE: I created custom books for a large number of agencies with a special page added for an agent to customize the gift of the book with their names, his comments to them, and his name and signature. It worked very well for anyone to use my book.

The second meeting

Let's get something out of the way right up front. Most agents want to get the sale closed at the second meeting. The needs assessment system did that; and LEAP could do it too. But I never did unless they were so ready that they pushed me to do so.

I heard plenty of stories from other agents, and sales representatives in Hawaii, that when they pushed for the sale at the second meeting, they spent a lot of time handling objections on why the prospect didn't need their products.

Here is what Zig Ziglar has to say about that, "Every sale has five basic obstacles: no need, no money, no hurry, no desire, no trust."

And the majority of all sales training is how to overcome objections. Because I had no training, I didn't know that. Instead, I had a much better way.

As I mentioned, I told my prospect right up front that there were three meetings in my process. Patience was my trademark.

"Patience is a virtue"
- Attributed to William Langland, circa 1360-87

During the second meeting, using LEAP charts and the data collected, I forecast the result of all of the things my prospects were doing; their pensions, IRAs, savings, current life insurance, stocks and bonds; everything.

Then I forecast their current expenses and between it all, calculated the velocity of money moving through their entire budget. Almost always, it was negative; but if it was positive it would be by only a very small amount.

I did this assuming all prospects lived to retirement. Since most of them didn't like the picture LEAP forecast for them, the next thing I would do is have the husband die (could be the wife) because back then it was still a male dominated workforce. When both worked, I would show the impact of either one dying.

But no matter what, for nearly everyone it was a really dreary picture; both alive and especially with a death.

I then closed that meeting asking them how they liked that picture and if they wanted to change it. Everyone, and I do mean everyone, wanted to change it.

I told them that together, and only with their total agreement, would I show them a way to make the changes to accomplish what they really wanted for their future at our next meeting.

The third meeting

Because they didn't like the picture they had seen at the prior meeting, the next question a prospect would ask would be how they could change that outcome. What did they need to change?

Here was my secret. I simply asked them what they wanted to achieve (referring to the original goals they had told me) and what they thought they needed to do to achieve it.

LEAP had a direct way of repositioning assets so that nearly every prospect could acquire all of the life insurance he or she needed, "…without taking one dime out of their pocket."

I did that for all but one of my clients. Their income was so low that the bottom line came down to drinking one less case of Coca-Cola a month. Yes, a case of soda.

They were veracious consumers of Coca-Cola. They had cases stacked up in their house. The husband made a very modest salary and she was a stay at home mom with two children. They had a total of $8,000 of life insurance, but they wanted $50,000.

I made that happen for them – all they had to do was give up one can of Coke a day.

One can a day, seven days a week.

Issues that LEAP brought to light

I discovered that using the LEAP system educated my clients on where their money went both good and bad. By doing that, they were empowered to make changes; changes they wanted, not what I told them to do.

Here is a list of the bad:

1. Saving money in a savings account. At that time interest rates were at 6% to 7%; but it was taxable.

2. Paying too much for car insurance. Nearly everyone had $100 deductible; and they would have thousands of dollars in

49

liquid assets from savings accounts or brokerage accounts or cash value of life insurance. They were insuring a risk they could assume

3. Having more than 2-3 life insurance policies was wasting money on the annual policy fees. I once found a client with 11 policies for a total death benefit of $18,000. He wanted $100,000. I pointed out that paying $50/$60 per year from his premiums on 11 policy fees was $500+ that was gone. That amount alone plus his current premiums would fund the policy he wanted. Not one dime was taken from his pocket.

4. Not having an IRA. This was stunning. At this time in the tax code, anyone with less than $100,000 of income could have an IRA. It was totally deductible and tax deferred. This alone could bring extra money to a household that had cash in savings assets and/or discretionary income.

5. Everyone but one client was woefully underinsured.

Here is a list of the good:

1. About half of my clients had significant dollars in savings accounts. Moving that to an IRA created windfall tax savings.

2. Nearly everyone with substantial savings/cash assets had $100 deductible car insurance. I would ask them when they last had an accident. Some would say never; some once in the past decade. I then pointed out that going to a $500 deductible would lower their car insurance by about $150 per year so that in three years they could save enough to cover an accident, and from then on be money ahead forever. This savings became cash flow to buy life insurance.

3. For nearly 80% of my clients, I convinced them to create a single policy, often with added rider coverage for their spouse

and children, and not pay any more premium than the amount they were currently paying on multiple policies. The savings in policy fees alone created future cash value in my company's policy beyond any amount their current policies were going to reach. I even found small whole life policies with low fixed interest (3%) and when I pointed that out it would make them angry. They felt taken and wanted to change that for sure.

4. I placed nearly half of all my prospects into an IRA. This boosted their future net worth and the tax deductible savings went to either life insurance or other brokerage accounts. Or it gave some clients extra money for household expenses. The biggest obstacle raised about doing an IRA was they simply did not understand how an IRA worked. Once they clearly understood the long-term investment value and the current tax savings, IRAs were easy to place.

5. The above four good things solved every one of my clients being underinsured. I placed life insurance on 90% of my clients by meeting number three. And I never used whole life – only universal life –either portfolio or variable.

LEAP and my simply strategy of asking the prospect what they wanted over their lifetime and showing them how to attain their personal and financial goals resulted in my being a superb salesman.

True life sales stories

The following are actual cases that occurred in my brief time working with individual prospects in personal sales.

<u>My mother has to see this.</u>

I met a young couple who had no children and both worked. He was 32 and she was 31. They had a solid upper middle class income, owned a home, and drove two recent model cars.

They also had $25,000 in a credit union share savings account funded with a monthly deduction directly from each of their paychecks, and, of course, $100 deductible car insurance.

They had no life insurance on her and only a $5,000 Lutheran Brotherhood policy on him that his mother had bought when he was ten. It had about $2,500 of cash value and a small annual premium that he was paying.

They were intensely proud of their success and didn't want to pay me a single extra cent from their budget. So I gave them the LEAP challenge saying, "If I can get each of you a $250,000 life insurance policy and not take one dime out of your cash flow, will you do business with me?"

His wife was already sold on their desire to have more coverage; but he was a bit feisty towards me. But when I offered that challenge he bit.

"If you can do that," he said, "I will buy the life insurance for both of us."

Then he added with a smirk, "But I don't think you can."

I then proceeded to convert his policy into a new one, and create a premium equal to what he put into the credit union; and likewise, I did the same for her. Startled, he said that didn't make sense, he wanted that money.

I showed him the LEAP forecast for his credit union account (after-tax) versus the insurance policies and of course there was a much greater value at age 65 even if he cashed them in and paid income taxes. At this point he began paying close attention to my proposal.

Next, I had him increase his auto insurance deductibles on two cars and that made about a $300 a year change. He retorted that he didn't want to do that saying, "What if I have a wreck. Now I'd have to pay more out of my pocket."

I shot right back with, "When did you have your last wreck?"

Proudly he fired back, "I have never had a wreck."

His wife laughed seeing how I had trapped him and offered that she too had never had a wreck.

I added up the annual savings for the past ten years, $3,000, and showed him how much money he had wasted. And of course, I pointed out that he had saved enough in the credit union to buy a new car if he wanted.

I also pointed out that he would only pay the deductible if it was his fault!

With that he gave up. The auto insurance savings became a credit to me and went into his credit union account on my forecast.

Next, I had him take out $4,000 from his credit union and put $2,000 into IRAs for each of them. He admitted that he had never done that because he didn't understand IRAs and didn't trust anybody that sold them.

But once again, after I fully explained them and showed the difference in future value of the IRA versus the taxable savings, I had him trapped in my challenge.

Long and short, I sold two IRAs, two life insurance policies and ended up with him still making a savings contribution to his credit union. The LEAP forecast of his future net worth was triple where we started. They were both very happy.

And then he said, "I need to call me mother and tell her what we're doing."

My heart sank. He went to the phone, a wall phone right there in the kitchen, dialed his mother and I heard his side of the conversation as follows:

"Yes, mom, he is an insurance agent."

"Yes, mom, he's with Lutheran Brotherhood."

"Yes, mom, he wants me to convert that policy you gave me twenty years ago."

He hung up the phone and said we had to go see his mother.

Now I distinctly recall this as it was on a Sunday afternoon, as he would not see me during the week. I further recall this because when I was asking for the appointment he joked and said, "I bet you don't work on Sunday's"

I said, "What time shall I be there."

Anyway, to make my now short story longer, we left his house and I followed in my car to his mother's house.

After I explained to his mother what I had proposed and why converting his policy was in his best interest, and of course saying how wonderful it was that she had purchased that policy for him over twenty years ago, she took an immediate liking to me.

She shared with me how hard it had been to pay for five insurance policies over the years on her five children. She was a long-time widow (her husband had been killed in a railroad work accident) and she felt she had to give her children something for their future back then.

"Today," she said, "I have nothing to leave my five children. I rent my house and when I die my indemnity pension from the railroad ends too."

Then she asked me, "How much would it cost to get a $25,000 policy to leave for my five children. I am sixty-three and I think I am in good health."

I wrote it up, and she got it. She also referred me to another son who lived in Nevada. All in all I made four life insurance policy sales that day (plus two IRAs).

My fear that mom was going to squelch my sale caught me totally off guard; you just have to go with the flow as you never know what will happen in sales.

"Make a customer, not a sale."
- Katherine Barchetti

Silver dollars and Mason jars.

One of the key things about me was I could pivot and change at a moment's notice. I had to do that as a pilot and a staff officer during my military career. That strength paid me often, but this story was one of the most unusual situations I ever had.

I had made an appointment to visit a Green Card client. On the phone she told me she was divorced and had three children, ages 3, 5 and 7. She told me she didn't make much money and lived with her parents at this time.

On arrival at her house her father met me at the door and said he wanted to talk with me first. We went into the kitchen and he introduced me to his daughter and his wife. Then his daughter excused herself to go upstairs to be with her children.

Father went right to it. He had given her the Lutheran Brotherhood policy she had and knew it was not enough. He and mother were very concerned about their grandchildren as their daughter was only able to work night shifts at a casino.

"What could they do to help?" he asked.

About then the coffee pot began to whistle and mother went to the stove. She apologized that they used instant coffee and asked if that was alright with me.

"Of course it is," I said but quickly added, "just black."

With that she opened a cabinet door, a door that went all the way to the kitchen ceiling, and I saw the top shelf filled with rows of Mason jars and glittering with silver coins.

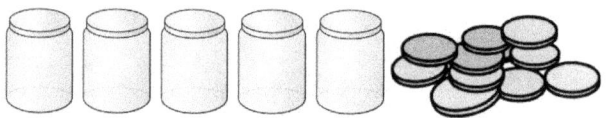

Father indicated that the daughter's husband had been a "no good blankety-blank" and would never be seen again. If their daughter were to die, they would have to raise the children.

Right up front he told me they wanted more life insurance on their daughter – so I just asked, "How much do you think you want?"

"One hundred thousand," he replied.

I mentioned that the daughter would have to sign the application but that he and mother should be the owners.

"Perfect," he replied.

I began the paperwork and shortly he called his daughter to come down and sign as the insured. I told her she would receive a call in a day or two for a simple medical exam right here at the house if that was okay with her.

She left and once more the cabinet was opened to get some cookies and I then commented on the Mason jars.

Turns out they went all the way around the top shelf of the entire kitchen cabinet and more were on the next shelf down.

Mother told me they had been saving silver dollars and silver half-dollars from change and keeping them to give to their grandchildren someday (they did say they weren't real silver as all of those type coins were long gone from circulation).

I replied that seemed like a great way to save, but commented that they did not earn any interest that way. Grandfather said he understood, but didn't know what they should do.

Hmmm. Do you think I had an idea?

Shortly, three applications for three grandchildren were completed and daughter came down and signed approval, but again, the two grandparents were the owners.

I had pointed out that the internal cost of life insurance on children was negligible and at current interest rates and IRS rules only about 2 ½ years of premiums could even be paid into each policy. I then gave them an idea.

I said that until the grandchildren turned 16. they (the grandparents) owned the policies.

But if the grandchildren were never were told about the policies they could just keep those policies on a closet shelf.

Then, when the grandchildren grew up, each policy would have a significant amount of cash value and be paid up for life.

It would make a wonderful wedding present.

For the bride and groom.

They loved that idea. They settled on $100,000 face per child. I told them to simply pay a first year premium equal to the IRS 7-pay amount and do the same the next year. After that the insurance company would tell them how much, if any, they could pay into the policy in future years.

Based on my illustration they could not pay anymore after the third year until the child was about eighteen. Even then it was paid-up for life.

When grandpa saw how small the premiums were for 2 ½ years he said they would make those payments and just keep saving more coins as they enjoyed doing that. The value of the coins would be a future gift for the children.

We all had a good laugh about the coins and how such a simple act of saving coins from change had become the basis for such an important plan for their family.

I felt really good that night. I had brought security and happiness to this family. One stop and six happy people as the grandchildren would be happy someday when they received those policies all paid-up.

"Try not to become a person of success, but try to become a person of value."

- Albert Einstein.

<u>The airline pilot</u>

I love this story. It was so true of so many of my prospects, but this one took some extra energy and ingenuity on my part.

He was a pilot for a regional airline based in Las Vegas. He had a good salary but only $100,000 of group term insurance and a single $25,000 policy with us.

Both he and his wife were second marriages; he was 44 and she was 42. They had no children at home and she did not work.

After my analysis, which I did on the second meeting, it was pretty clear that they would have adequate retirement income because they had no college expenses, etc.

But clearly, he was seriously underinsured, and he would not accept that outcome as he put up every objection I had ever heard.

Then I decided to kill him off. He grudgingly agreed to my doing that and I began as follows:

"Mrs. Widow, I am sorry for your loss and have brought you a check from my insurance company for $25,000. I understand you also received a check for $100,000 from his group policy."

I had to nudge her a bit, but she caught on and replied, "Yes, thank you. I really will need that."

"Mrs. Widow, since you are not working, and based on your mortgage and other cash needs, how long do you think this will last?"

She replied that she had not given that much thought and asked me how to figure that.

I brought out the LEAP forecast and removed his salary and showed her the money would only last about ten years.

"Ten years," she said. "What will I do then?"

"I suppose you will have to find a job," I replied.

About then Mr. Pilot started to talk but I cut him off saying he was dead. It was her problem to solve, I pointed out, not his.

She began to think and I asked her about her work history. She replied that she had actually never had a job as she had raised three children in her prior marriage, had a bad divorce with no support as the kids were of age, and now she had no idea what she could do.

I opened my mouth and said, "Given you need to keep the house, Las Vegas has lots of jobs like a waitress or other service position."

I then added, "Or maybe you could be a maid in a hotel?"

Mr. Pilot jumped in then by saying, "OK. I get it. I will buy the extra hundred thousand dollars you proposed."

She turned to him, smiled sweetly and said, "Thank you honey. You don't have to sleep on the couch tonight."

<u>The beauty queen</u>

This is my favorite story of all. I had called on this man during my first two weeks as an agent in January, 1987.

He was 42 and held a good position as a career civil servant. I had gathered all his data at our first meeting albeit he was reluctant to do so. He had three times salary in group insurance and a single old whole policy for $5,000 with our company. He had the civil service retirement plan and he owned his home.

In my mind I decided to make this a two meeting call and he agreed to a follow-up meeting in one week.

As it turned out, Gregg, my general agent, came to Las Vegas the next week and went with me on this follow-up meeting.

He met us at the door, I introduced Gregg, and he escorted us into the kitchen. They had one of those old style six seat kitchen tables with chrome trim and a green marble patterned Formica top. It was right out of the 1950's.

On my prior meeting his wife was not present, but tonight she was there. His wife was gorgeous – truly beautiful.

He sat at one end of this table, I sat at the other end, Gregg was to my left and his wife sat to his left. The other two chairs were obviously empty.

I made my presentation and concluded he clearly had a need for some additional life insurance. I stated he could use the $5,000 policy with us to jump-start a variable contract that would be a great addition to his retirement funds. And of course, should he die prematurely, it would protect his wife with a continued income.

After making my recommendations, he asked one or two questions and then became silent. I knew from past experience that when someone does that to keep my mouth shut and let him speak first.

Finally he spoke, and what a shock I had with what he said, and I quote, "Mr. High, look at my wife. She is beautiful. If I were to die she could marry anyone she wanted to and be taken care of. I don't need any additional insurance."

I was stunned. I slapped my right hand down so hard on that table it shook. Then I shook my finger at him and said,

"Sir, you insult me and you insult your wife. Who are you to say how she might feel if you were to die suddenly. You have no right to say her future support would be to marry someone else!"

Gregg slunk down in his chair, this man gave me an awful look, and his wife turned to him shooting daggers from her eyes at him and firmly and loudly said, "You buy that insurance and you buy it now!"

Then she got up and left the room leaving us all in a stunned silence.

After about thirty seconds had passed, he looked at me and said with venom in his voice, "What do I need to sign?"

I quickly asked him the necessary questions, filled out the application and handed it across the table for him to sign.

He tossed it back to me and stood up. Gregg and I took our cue and headed for the door.

In the car Gregg said to me, "What on earth got into you to say that to him?"

I replied, "Gregg, I am a retired colonel. I am a human being. I will not sit and allow anyone to disparage me or his wife or any other person. I don't need a commission so badly that I would allow such uncalled for conduct."

The medical exam was completed by the para-med service and once I received the approved policy I made a call and set an appointment to bring it to him. It had no additional delivery requirements which I was thrilled to see.

I rang his doorbell. In a moment he opened the door and asked me if the envelope in my hand was his policy.

I said it was and started to move forward when he grabbed the envelope right out of my hand and slammed the door in my face.

You have to remember that at that point in time I was truly a rookie in the life insurance business, but very comfortable meeting people and making presentations. And I sure didn't need any more of this guy.

I wonder how long he spent sleeping on the couch.

> "Sales are contingent upon the attitude of the salesman, not the attitude of the prospect."
>
> – William Clement Stone

<u>The largest sale I ever made</u>

I met with a man for our second visit and as I reviewed his LEAP booklet, it became crystal clear he didn't need to do a thing. He had adequate life insurance (a Lutheran Brotherhood policy plus more with other companies), and a substantial net worth.

"Of course," I said, "I could recommend you move some of your investments to our mutual funds, but candidly that would be more for my benefit than for yours."

He nodded his head, smiled and thanked me. Then I left.

A week later my phone rang. "Mr. High," be began, "when I met with you I pretty much knew I didn't need anything, I just wanted to confirm that."

I said I was happy to oblige.

Then he continued, "I have a very good friend who really does need your services. I know I can trust you and I have given him your name as someone he can trust too."

He then gave me his friend's phone number and I thanked him for giving me this opportunity and assured him I would treat his friend just as I would treat myself.

When I met his friend, it quickly became clear he had a mess. He had high income and no personal life insurance (only group term at work). Worse, he had a brokerage account which clearly had been getting a lot of churning.

I made the single biggest sale of my personal sales career with him; a $500,000 life policy and $600,000 to mutual funds.

> "You will get all you want in life if you help enough other people get what they want."
>
> - Zig Ziglar

<u>Final client meetings</u>

The bad part of selling so many policies was that I had to deliver them. Being a Lutheran Brotherhood agent was a one-man show.

I did most of my deliveries on Saturdays as well as sales calls. I often had up to eight appointments on Saturdays.

But deliveries took time and became a drag on my production. By March my follow-up deliveries and service calls had reduced my first meetings by one-half.

I was alone and not prepared for such a level of overall activity. During the daytime I had few opportunities to make house calls. Las Vegas was a two shift town and the night shift slept during daytime.

From time to time I had meetings at 2am after the casino crowd left work. It was a weird feeling to go to someone's home at that time of night and have coffee and cookies and visit with prospects who were relaxed and wanting to talk about their financial futures.

Is it bedtime yet?

<u>Lessons learned</u>

1. The single most important of all. Don't tell people what they need and then try a hard sell. Let them tell you what they want.

> "People don't buy for logical reasons. They buy for emotional reasons."
> - *Zig Ziglar*

2: The most important thing I learned about people is that they want to believe in you.

You must return that favor by believing in them. You must put their best interest forward at all times.

You must not care about the sale and what it pays you; you must care about the consequences to your prospects if they don't buy. They can tell if you are a money hungry agent right away.

If you have made the case for the product(s), especially death benefit needs, let them reach their own conclusion. Keep your cool and your mouth shut.

> "I like to think of sales as the ability to gracefully persuade, not manipulate, a person or persons into a win-win situation."
> - Bo Bennett

If they say no, accept it. But then, ask that one additional question, something that came out during your two or three visits with them.

I call it the Columbo moment (after the bumbling detective played by Peter Falk in the TV series Columbo from 1968-78 and again from 1989-2003).

Believe me, you will know it. There is always something the prospect said that will now cause them to reassess why they are saying no.

> "The questions you ask are more important than the things you could ever say."
>
> - Tom Freese

3: Tell stories about others. Have a story about a similar situated family like the one you are talking with who did what you have recommended to them, hopefully from a decision that they may have even proposed.

Then have another story about a similar couple who did the opposite and share what happened to them.

Then ask the prospect, and especially if his wife is sitting there, which story will be their story? Which one do they want to have told about them?

> "In the South, we tell stories. We tell stories if you're in a sales position, if you're in a retail position, you lure your customer by telling a story. You just do."
>
> - Tate Taylor

4: Expect the unexpected. Then use it to your advantage. Mason jars have been known to come with lots of good things in them. And never ever accept insults or condescending language. It could just be a test of your character.

> "The successful people are the ones who can think up things for the rest of the world to keep busy at."
>
> - Don Marquis

5. You have to know the sales process. LEAP was a systematic way to sell by showing the prospect mathematical forecasts and then pulling out the emotions of what they told the prospect.

LEAP was hard work. Many of the older agents failed using it probably because they truly couldn't handle the math; possibly because they didn't want to work at it; and most likely because it could make your head hurt.

Candidly it was outside of the average agent's ability to adapt. Eventually it was automated and began to look more like the prior needs analysis system, just had more numbers for input and more for output.

"Don't wish it were easier, wish you were better."

- Jim Rohn

"It's supposed to be hard. If it were easy, everyone would do it."

- Tom Hanks in A League of Their Own

Chapter 7
Failure; and another fork in the road

Sunday, July 12, 1987, at approximately 7:30pm, I threw up while making a cold call.

I had reached the point where the very sight of the telephone in my office caused my stomach to knot up. I could no longer go on.

Moira, my wife, was very concerned about me, and us, especially since she had lost her job at a jewelry store in Caesar's Palace in June.

The owners of the store were not doing well and decided they would come back and work the store themselves. As a result they let two employees go, and Moira was the last one hired, first one fired.

Financially I was barely making it compared to what I had expected as a corporate junior executive. The last two months of my insurance earnings had slipped and with all of this on my mind and hers, I was at my wits end. I was getting desperate.

3:00am and the phone rings

There is an old religious expression that when God closes a door, he also opens a window. I am not keen on such sayings, but six hours after I threw up, my bedside phone was ringing.

I was not unusual to get calls at odd hours when in the air force, as the organization I oversaw at the base before I retired was a worldwide operation. But since retiring from the air force I had not had a late night call.

I awoke, answered, and heard a voice say, "Lynn, this is Rich."

At first I thought it was my friend Rich from Northrop (the one who I would have worked with) so I said, "Yes, Rich, what has happened?"

He replied, "Can you hear me? I am in Saudi and can barely hear you."

I was now perplexed, sat up and said much louder, "Who is this?"

"This is Rich. Rich Frienmuth. I worked for you at Nellis two years ago. Do you remember me?"

I replied I did as my memory at 3am slowly came into focus. He had been our F-5 test pilot and had retired and started a Swenson's Ice Cream Parlor. Then I lost track of him.

Rich continued, "Lynn, Faisal wants to speak to you."

In a moment I heard a voice say, "Lean, Lean, this is Faisal. I want you work for me. Rich will tell you details."

My memory was now clear. Faisal was a Saudi pilot I had flown with ten years ago and he always called me Lean instead of Lynn.

Rich was back on the phone and told me all about being in Saudi and working for Colonel Faisal. He said he had told Faisal he had heard I had retired a few months ago, and Faisal asked him to call me. There was an open position as the advisor to the commander (Faisal) at the Saudi air base where Rich was located.

Rich said if I was interested I should call a number at Lear-Siegler in Oklahoma City and use both his and Faisal's names with them.

I wrote the number down and talked with Rich a few more minutes and then rolled back into bed and went to sleep.

In the morning, I called the number in Oklahoma. I knew all about the advisor positions in Saudi Arabia as many a colonel had been there before. It paid well and most enjoyed it.

After talking about thirty minutes with Lear-Siegler, I was tentatively hired. All I had to do was have a background security check for Secret (which would be no issue), pass a medical exam, and get a visa approved. This would all take about thirty days.

I had made a tough decision. But at that moment, it was what I needed to do.

One final call

I waited about a couple of days before I called Gregg. When I told him he was shocked. He said he was flying to Vegas immediately; would I pick him up at the airport?

I agreed. After he arrived we drove back to my house with little conversation. When we arrived I poured two stiff drinks and our discussion began.

He was shocked. He didn't realize how bad it had become for me. I had followed his advice and rented an executive business suite in an office building with a common receptionist, but I told him I rarely met people there.

I had also held several seminars with fair success, but the cold calling of non-orphans had simply become so oppressive for me that I could not mentally or physically continue.

He realized that my mind was made up and then we talked as friends for a while. Moira brought in some snacks and sat with us and finally she cried telling him how stressed we both were.

Gregg accepted this as the best for us both. We both drove him back to the airport for a late flight back to Phoenix.

On August 18, 1987, I departed Las Vegas via New York for Khamis Mushayt Royal Saudi Air Base in the land of sand.

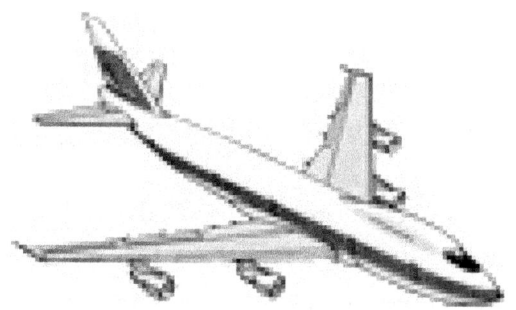

Three records

According to Gregg, I had set three records with Lutheran Brotherhood during my 6 ½ months with them in 1987.

The first was that I made $18,000 in commissions and allowances during my first month. No rookie had every done that before. They could not even pay me as the largest check they could write to a rookie was for $9,999.

The second was policy size. I had sold 66 life policies for a total of $9,600,000 face value. That is $145,000 per policy, a record at that time.

Third, I broke the first year rookie's total earnings. I had made $50,301 in only 6 ½ months. No new guy before me had ever made that much money in his entire first year (12 months).

On top of all of that, I had averaged an 80% closing ratio on Green Card clients; and a 50% closing ratio on other clients (ratio based on at least one sale per family seen).

But for me I had failed – I didn't feel like a record holder. And you know what's really funny?

I hadn't made it past one-fourth of the Green Card orphans. If I had just focused on them I probably would have made triple the amount of money that I did. I would have then had more time to develop a system for cold calls.

I just needed someone to show me a better way.

Lessons learned

1. I loved personal selling of life insurance; I hated making cold calls. I let them defeat me.

> "If you learn from defeat, you haven't really lost."
> - Zig Ziglar

2. Cold calls are the lifeblood of any type of sales. If you can't hack them, you need to find another career. I did just that in 1987; a decision I still regret to this day.

What I needed was a telemarketer to help me get through that trying time in my life insurance sales career.

Eventually, as you will soon learn when you read on, I came out on the other side, but it took a couple of years.

> "The majority of men meet with failure because of their lack of persistence in creating new plans to take the place of those which fail."
> - Napoleon Hill

3. Ask for referrals. It may seem awkward at first, but be proud of your work. Asking clients to share their success with others is a lot better than cold calling – and it may lead to the best prospects you will ever have.

> "In sales, a referral is the key to the door of resistance."
> - Bo Bennett

Part 3: Bank owned life insurance selling

I had banished myself to Saudi Arabia. After about a month I began to recover my attitude through three activities.

First, I learned to SCUBA dive. Diving in the Red Sea was fantastic, albeit it is one of the most shark infested waters on the planet.

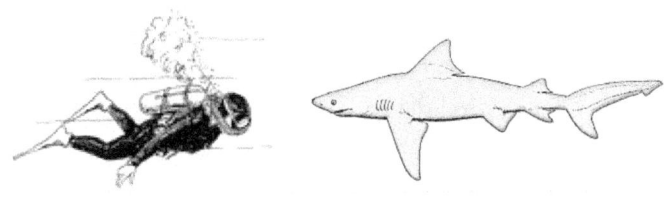

The good news was they were well feed as the water teemed with fish. Lucky for me as I once had a 6-7 foot black tip bump into me going around a large brain-head coral in fifteen feet of water. He stopped, turned and swam away.

The coral reefs in the Saudi half of the Red Sea were probably the best in the world as rarely did a human touch them. And the dive clubs had agreements to not touch or break the coral other than a few reefs designated for spearfishing.

Second, my site manager had also tried to sell life insurance when he retired from the air force and had a personal library of about 100 books on selling. He gave me the entire collection and I read them over time. From these books I began to learn of the many errors I had made in cold calling.

Third, I had endless time on my hands. I lived alone in a three bedroom house with full maintenance, both inside and out.

I worked from 7am to 2pm beginning with breakfast every day with the commander and his senior staff for the first two hours, then at 11am I had lunch in the flight line chow hall, and at 2pm I headed home. Reading became the primary outlet for my time.

Every other weekend was diving, and on several others Rich and I drove out into the desert to look at the stars.

Astronomy had been a childhood hobby, and at Khamis Mushayt we were at 6,700 feet altitude and the desert air was very dry. When there was no moon it was total darkness in the desert as there were no manmade lights visible for miles.

Lying on a cot in total darkness made me feel like I could just reach out and touch each and every star. Over the year I saw every visible planet and a one comet.

Other than a couple of bouts of abject loneliness, I recovered my ego from my defeat about making cold calls. I studied the books I had been given and learned from my past in order to be ready if I ever had another opportunity to sell anything again.

Another fork in the road shows up

On Friday morning, April 22, 1988, the phone in my house rang. As a point of order, Friday and Saturday were our days off as the Islamic week in Saudi is Sunday to Thursday, with Friday being the Islamic holy day.

The voice on the phone was our site manager. He proceeded to tell me that my wife Moira's visa had been approved and that she could come over at any time. I thanked him and said I would call her with the news.

Actually, I was pissed off. I had been in Saudi for eight months, all alone, when I had originally been told that my wife would be joining me in ninety days.

I had learned in November that our company had to re-bid their five-year contract with the Saudi air force and if awarded, it would be effective February 1, 1988. I also learned they had stopped all visa requests until they had won the bid and would not begin processing them until the new contract was in force.

If they did not win renewal, everyone would be returned home at company expense. I was not happy when I learned all about that.

Moira had sold our house in Las Vegas and had all our furniture put in storage by the air force. It had taken two months to sell the house after which she stayed with a friend expecting to come to Saudi any time (ninety days from my departure).

When I realized that her visa was delayed, she moved to Cancun, Mexico, to sell timeshares. The money from the sale of the house and our two cars was enough to keep things going.

His call was good news; but as I said I was P.O.'d.

And then the phone rang again

At about 3am that same Friday night (now actually Saturday) my phone rang again. I was slightly annoyed being awakened at that time, but I picked it up.

"Hello Lynn," the voice said clearly in perfect English, "this is Roger Beverage."

I kind of gulped hard. I knew him well but had no idea why he would be calling. I said, "Hello," and he continued.

"Did you receive the package I sent you?"

I replied that I had not but that mail here often took two weeks. I asked when he had sent it.

"Ten days ago," he replied. He confirmed my address and asked when I received it to I please call him. We chatted a couple more minutes and then hung up.

Calls between Saudi and the USA in those days were crystal clear, but for me to call outside Saudi I had to arrange a time with the base operator to call the outside number. When the phone was answered there, the base operator rang my house.

A bit cumbersome but in Saudi the government controlled all communication with the outside world.

On Sunday (our Monday) I went to the post office after work and a package from Roger was there. It had a bunch of brochures about a program called Bank Compensation Strategies and their concept for selling life insurance to banks.

After reading it several times, I realized this was a great idea. That evening, morning in Oklahoma City where Roger was the executive director of the Oklahoma Bankers Association, I set up a call to him. The ensuing conversation was very intriguing.

He wanted me to come back and join his team to sell this insurance to Oklahoma banks. He had been the Nebraska Director of Banking when this program was approved in that state (he and I were long-time friends having both gone to college at the same time in Lincoln) and it had just been approved in Oklahoma.

He said he had signed a contract with Bank Compensation Strategies for the bankers association's insurance agency to handle sales there.

I listened and said I was very interested and that I would be back in the USA the third week of June for one month's vacation. I would arrange time to spend with him in Oklahoma and decide.

I asked if he could send more information about this idea and the company, which he did. Although I didn't mind living in Saudi, my work was not a challenge and the long absence from my wife had soured me on being there.

It seemed God was opening another window and I at least needed to give it my full consideration.

Vacation

I landed at Dulles airport west of Washington, D.C. on June 24th after an all day and night of travel. My sister, Linda, met me and we went to her home in Culpeper, Virginia.

The next day my wife arrived from Mexico and we then went to my sister's ski lodge at Wintergreen in the Blue Ridge Mountains. After several days we returned to spend two more days with my sister, and then we flew to Nebraska.

After a week with my mother (my father had died in 1985) and my older sister and brother, along six nieces and nephews, Moira and I headed to Oklahoma City.

We stayed with Roger and his wife Paula at their home in Edmond. Paula was a classmate of my youngest sister and I had known her and her family since childhood.

Roger and I spent several days together talking about his ideas for this opportunity for me. One thing I will always remember is when Roger asked how much money I needed he was very surprised. He had no idea they paid that well in Saudi.

We worked out a base salary with benefits and then a draw against commissions to give me the total amount of cash flow I needed. The draw would be a debt owed by me if I did not meet the goals we set.

He then met with the executive committee of the association and they approved his proposed plan.

One point I recall him telling me was the directors asking him if he was okay with having an employee who would have the potential to make more than he did. After all he was the highest ranking officer of the thirty-some employees of the association; and bankers believed in a pecking order for pay based on position.

He told me his reply was, "If Lynn can earn it he can have it, because if he does we make a good share of it too."

And that settled that. I would return to Saudi and terminate in August after I had stayed one year in order to claim my overseas tax exemption.

I left Saudi Arabia on August 18, 1988, and I never looked back.

Chapter 8
On the road again

On the road again
Just can't wait to get on the road again
The life I love is makin' music with my friends
And I can't wait to get on the road again

- excerpt from On the Road Again by Willie Nelson

On Wednesday, September 1, 1988, I became an employee of the Oklahoma Bankers Association Insurance Agency and began my third and final sales career.

To jump start my new sales endeavor, Roger Beverage, the executive director of the association and president of the insurance agency, thus my boss, had held several regional meetings over the prior summer with bankers where he outlined the basic concept of the agency's new offering of bank owned life insurance to them.

He had received 38 reply cards from attending bankers who said they wanted to learn more about it. They had checked the box that said, "Please have Lynn High give me a call."

Whew…no cold calling to get me started here.

But then Roger, who was giving me lots of mentoring about working with bankers said, and I quote, "Bankers are easy to see but hard to sell."

Hmmm. That sounded right down my alley.

Bankers, and especially those in the small community banks located across the 400 towns and cities across the state, literally sat at their desks waiting for someone like me to walk in, and again I quote Roger, "…to steal money from them."

I even heard the expression,"… that it was easier to rob a bank with a pen than with a gun."

In other words, bankers have to listen to every idea for a loan and then sort the good ones from the bad. A banker's job is to make loans; but he is graded on how well he does collecting them.

Bank presidents/CEOs and operations officers and CFO's were called on almost daily by a bevy of sales representatives hawking some new service or product used by community banks. For example, copy machines and paper, checks and check processing services, ATM machines, loan software, etc.

In short, it was the banker's job to listen to all these people and their ideas because, from time to time, a really good idea came by that could improve the bank's bottom line; and they had to know about all of them to choose something useful.

The good news for me was that the only banker I wanted to meet with was the president/CEO. What I had to sell required approval by the full board of directors, and the president controlled the agenda and access.

Lastly, Roger told me that the way a banker says no is to nod his head up and down in agreement with your proposal while mumbling something like, "…uh huh, uh huh, that sounds like it could be done, etc." Then he would tell you it would require the loan or executive committee to approve it.

Later, when that committee said no, the banker was off the hook to that potential robber—I mean borrower.

Trip to Minneapolis

On September 14, Roger and I flew to Minneapolis, Minnesota, to meet Mr. Larry Hendrickson, the owner of Bank Compensation Strategies and creator of bank owned life insurance.

Roger told me that Larry had opposed his hiring me. Larry said he had tried a few retired military officers and they just couldn't adapt to being a beggar (I mean salesman) versus being in charge as a commander. And besides, he told Roger, it appeared that I had only been a salesman for six months before and had failed at that.

Roger told Larry he would like me once he met me, and since the contract with Larry was with the agency and Roger was in charge of it, from Roger's perspective the deal was done.

With all of this in mind, Roger and I entered Larry Hendrickson's office at 8am, Tuesday, September 15, 1988, expecting to meet some resistance.

Larry was gracious to me and I decided to take the offensive in the meeting. I proceeded to tell him about my sales experience in Hawaii, which Roger knew little about.

I also brought a copy of my book, Pay Yourself First, autographed it right there and gave it to Larry. Then I told him all about my short time with Lutheran Brotherhood and why I had failed. I also mentioned my three records with them.

Larry was rather stunned. He pressed me on why I would quit them; and I went through the stress of cold calls and generally my sense of aloneness in my work in Las Vegas.

I assured him that I had studied during my year in Saudi and was prepared for this new opportunity.

Roger stepped in by repeating his prior statement that it was easy to see a banker, but hard to sell him. Larry acknowledged that was true. Roger outlined my prior military experience in briefing generals and their staff, being a speaker at seminars in Hawaii, and sales to my sister's doctor friends.

At this point Larry said he was impressed and promptly closed out having any issue with me working in his program with bankers.

Larry then admitted that he had engaged several hundred insurance agents as sales representatives of his company over the past two years and nearly all of them had failed too. Seems they all wanted to sell the product in two or three calls. They simply didn't know how to use a lengthy approval process and how to handle a board of directors.

Larry said the top two salesmen he had were a former bank loan officer named Rich Chapman, and a retired NFL all conference linebacker named Wally Hilgenberg, formerly of the Minnesota Vikings.

Both worked in his office and I met them that day. As the years unfolded Rich became a super friend of mine and Wally was always a team player and sales leader. They were both my early go-to guys for sales ideas and understanding banker's objections.

I spent another day and a half at Larry's office and learned all I could about the product, the process, and the paperwork it took to put the program in a bank.

The programs main focus was on supplemental executive retirement plans (salary continuation agreements) and director retirement plans (fee deferral agreements). These plans were then funded by the bank's purchase of a special single-premium life insurance product that Larry had convinced two insurance companies to design exclusively for banks.

I was in heaven. This looked like shooting fish in a barrel to me.

First sales call in Oklahoma

During the week after the trip to Minneapolis, I did a lot of work making folders and outlines on association letterhead and creating a true association driven product.

The Oklahoma Bankers Association had six people in the insurance agency, and another dozen in sales of non-insurance bank services. In short, we were all in sales.

The association had a graphics department with the ability to print anything I wanted. It also had a news clipping program with files on every bank that along with were two lobbyists could tell me everything I needed to know about a specific bank and the president before I even left the building.

I also made four phone calls to bankers from the cards Roger had previously collected and all four said, "Come on down."

I knew I was in the right place at last. On Monday, September 28, I walked into my first bank in El Reno, just west of Oklahoma City, with an appointment to see the president. He welcomed me (and I took the coffee black) and I gave him an overview of how this program worked.

> NOTE: I will not use any banker's name; only town/city names as a reference point. I do not want any banker to feel I misquoted him or in any way passed judgement on any one case or situation.

The bank's president was really intrigued. He was especially interested in the director retirement plan. As a means of creating a basic illustration of how it worked, I obtained his date of birth, whether he smoked, and the amount of his fee. In about half an hour I left with a future appointment in two weeks to go over an initial proposal with him.

Larry Hendrickson had cautioned me about telling bankers too much up front. This was a true process sale where bankers needed to learn to know me and trust me. Wow. Right out of my past experience.

I had determined that I would need a process and the following was my initial plan for my order of visits:

> Visit 1: Introduce myself and briefly outline the programs and how they worked generically. Find out which one might have the best appeal in this bank and then ask for only the president's age, whether he smoked, and the amount of his director's fee or salary. Set an appointment with him for two weeks in the future to outline that idea.

> Visit 2: Show the president the plan just for him and use the forecasts to outline the impact to the bank.

> If he liked it, ask for a census of all the directors or officers. Set an appointment for two weeks in the future for another proposal review.

Visit 3: Show the president the proposal for all of the directors (or officers), and if one of the other officers in the bank was a director, ask to have him to sit in; but none of the outside directors.

If they both liked it and thought it would work, then ask for another meeting in a week or two with a key director. A key director was someone knowledgeable in finance or accounting, open to new ideas, and on their executive committee.

Visit 4: Meet with the president and that one director and really work through the benefits, costs and other issues.

If that director liked it, ask if they wanted to present it to a committee of the board, such as the executive committee; or if they wanted their outside accounting firm to review it.

After the fourth visit, there was a key bridge that had to be crossed. This program was new and had almost no regulation other than a statutory limit on the amount of life insurance cash value a bank could hold. GAAP was the accounting standard; but some of the aspects were not clear. Many regional accounting firms did not agree with the opinions we had from our company's accounting firm and that had to be ironed out.

Visit 5: After a meeting with outside accountants, or the executive committee with a lawyer or CPA present, the next hurdle was a full board meeting.

Visit 6: I always asked the president to set me up for two board meeting presentations. The first board presentation was information only. In that way the directors could ask questions and not be under any obligation to approve or disapprove. I also made this very clear at the board meeting so the directors felt at ease to listen and ask questions.

Visit 6+: Often there would be an interim meeting with a key director or shareholder who had a background in law or accounting, or simply held the most clout with the other members.

I often met with this person between the first and second board presentation with the goal of winning him over. By doing so at the next board meeting I would ask his opinion on how I answered other directors' questions. It was a great way to triangulate from me to him, someone the other directors trusted.

Visit 7: The second board presentation at the following month's board meeting would be the approval meeting.

From this point forward many banks took an individualized route on implementation. If their CPA firm had not reviewed it they often required me to do that before they would actually finalize the bank board meeting minutes and actually give it a green light at their next meeting.

At this point being flexible was a key aspect of moving to a wire transfer of a million dollars or more of bank funds.

This was my game plan and it worked beautifully. But my problem quickly became that there were not enough days in a week to do it all.

I was awash in leads and banks moving the process forward.

Geography was not my friend

It didn't take me very long to have a calendar so full of appointments, nearly all follow-up, that I quickly began to run out of time. Oklahoma is a pretty big state when you drive a car; and then one day it hit me – I was a pilot.

This revelation occurred on Tuesday, February 14, 1989. I had made an appointment for a first call at a bank in Cherokee which is about three hours northwest of Oklahoma City. I left my house early as the appointment was for 10am.

NOTE: Before you wonder how I recall all of this I have a photographic memory. I can name dates and places and tell you where I sat in a restaurant ten years ago as if it's today. And before you think it is truly a gift, let me warn you it is also a curse.

I can relive almost any major event of my life by simply closing my eyes and seeing it in my mind's eye.

I also have dreams (or nightmares) reliving the past that drive me nearly crazy and I suffer from insomnia as a result.

I can also re-dream events of long ago and then write them down. Right now I could draw a floor plan of this bank from over twenty-five years ago and tell you the table in the lobby with the birthday cake sat.

But now back to my revelation. It was a very clear and beautiful February day. I hadn't really stopped to think about it, but the shortest highway to Cherokee was through Enid, and as I began to approach Enid I could see the little T-37 jet trainers in the sky.

Enid is where Vance Air Force Base is located and is where I went through pilot training and later was a T-38 instructor after my first combat tour in Vietnam.

91

The road alongside the base had an overpass with turnoffs for the main gate and as I crested it I saw a string of T-38 white rockets coming in from the north for practice landings.

I became so overwhelmed with memories that I had to pull over on the shoulder of the road as I began to weep. Yes, I sat in my car and wept.

This was the first time I came face to face with the reality that I once flew those very aircraft. After I left my air force career and lost my dream job I had been floundering around with my life (that was covered in part 1).

I finally composed myself and picked up my car phone. I drove a company owned car that after two months on the road the past fall I realized I needed a car phone and Roger agreed.

It was installed in the trunk and worked best in towns or on the top of a hill when in the countryside; but it opened up my ability to do more.

I dialed 411 and asked for Tinker AFB in Oklahoma City. When the base operator answered, I asked if they had a flying club. She transferred my call to the base commander's office.

I told them who I was and my question, and then heard someone in the background say that Colonel Weeks might know.

I asked the secretary if that was Wally Weeks, and when she said it was I asked to speak to him saying he would know me.

Wally had been a college classmate at the University of Nebraska and in my pilot training class at Enid.

After catching up with a quick, "… what have you been doing?" conversation, Wally told me they did not have an aero club on base, but there was a man in Guthrie, the first town north of Oklahoma City, named Glenn Crabtree who operated a flying club at the Guthrie airport.

Wally was a member and gave me Glenn's phone number and said I should use his name as a reference when I called him.

Birthday cake and happy bankers

I arrived at the bank in Cherokee and they were just starting a birthday celebration. It was the president's birthday and after cake and coffee we went into his office.

He loved my ideas. He had read about the program in an article I had written and published in the January edition of the bankers association's monthly magazine.

I wrote an article every other month and would get one or two calls from bankers from each one. Writing articles added to my reputation and legitimacy. I continued to do that for years to come.

By this time I was awash in leads and had not yet contacted half of the cards Roger had collected. I was in salesman's heaven; but I needed help. I needed more hands and more time.

Beating geography with a small plane

I called Glenn Crabtree on the drive back from Cherokee and scheduled a flight with him that coming Saturday. I quickly checked out in four of Glenn's planes including a twin engine.

I had banks to see in the furthest corners of the state and was running myself ragged; however, I quickly found that bankers loved to come to their local airport and pick me up. They would speak with pride about their airport and how it helped support their town's commerce.

I soon began making flights for day outings several times a month stopping to see two banks each day while covering all four corners of the state and even the panhandle area – and that was a long way to go even in an airplane.

Once more I was back in the saddle flying airplanes and I became a truly happy camper.

I finally found my calling in sales and returned to my first love of flying. I couldn't ask for a better situation.

Chapter 9
Why doesn't everybody do this?

One of my early calls was at a bank in Hollis, which is the last town in the southwest corner of the state.

NOTE: To repeat, I am not going to use actual banker's names. Some still work; many have retired; and I have a few stories that are not totally complimentary.

After my first visit, the president was very interested in the salary continuation plan. He was a highly experienced banker and had been recruited from an out of state bank six years before. He was in his mid-fifties, and this bank had a defined contribution pension plan. As a consequence, due to this age, he was not destined to get much from it for retirement.

Rather than using the pine box retirement plan, he felt his board would listen to my approach for a supplemental retirement plan to provide full retirement income for him.

At my second meeting, after he understood all of the accounting and how the life insurance funding worked to offset the costs, I will never forget him saying, and I quote, "Why wouldn't every bank do this?"

At that time I was of the same mindset, but Roger had warned me saying, "Bankers fall into three unique categories."

Then he continued with this summary:

One-third of them are innovators and will jump on every new idea right away;

One-third of them are sheep and watch the first third to see how they do with the new idea; and then, when they see it works they follow and do it too; and

The final one-third of them are just hard headed and generally don't want some outside salesperson telling them what they should do. And this attitude can also be applied to many directors.

I wondered about this last group and over time realized that they were the ones who did not have ATMs until the very end, did not pay their people a lot resulting in constant turn-over in their lending department as other banks would recruit their best, and they were the ones that would only send their people to training if the regulators made them do it. They were just hard headed.

Well that was okay with me – that left 280 banks to do business with.

Oklahoma's four corners

With sales leads almost pouring in, and follow-up meetings taking lots of travel time, joining the airplane club at Guthrie was a home run.

I soon was on my way making plane trips to the furthest banks while reserving the nearer banks for driving trips. Overall, I would spend 2-3 nights a week away from home and at least one day a week flying. But at this point, I had not closed one sale.

Larry Hendrickson decided I needed a pep talk and in March, 1989, he flew to Oklahoma for a three day visit. I really think he wanted to see if I was really worth a darn.

Apparently, in the past, he had charged agents for proposals and illustrations. Under the contract he made with Roger, he had agreed to not do so. When he came to the association to meet with Roger and me, he told us that I had been doing more proposals than anyone else but with no revenue.

I had a meeting with Roger every two weeks and an agency board meeting every month. I had kept everyone up to date on sales calls, number of repeat calls, etc. I had the status of every bank for Roger's review.

As Roger reviewed this with Larry his tone changed. Roger assured him that based on the experience he had had in Nebraska with Larry's program, the quick sale mentality of insurance agents actually ruined good bank prospects.

He showed Larry some of the board meeting presentations I had prepared and the marketing brochures and other literature I had created in our graphics department. Larry was not only impressed, he was humbled.

I showed Larry a map on my office wall that was 3'X7' and had a pin code for every bank I had set foot in. So far there were no red or green pins, but lots of white and blue. Again, he was impressed.

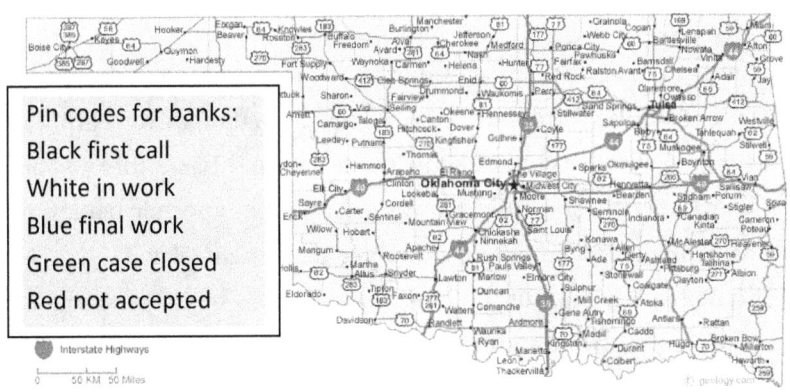

Pin codes for banks:
Black first call
White in work
Blue final work
Green case closed
Red not accepted

I had made two appointments for us the next day in the very southeast corner of the state in Broken Bow and Idabel. I rented a Beechcraft Bonanza to fly to them both, as it would have been a six hour drive each way by car on freeways and a two-lane road through the Ouachita forest. Larry agreed the airplane was a good idea.

Flying around the clouds

The night before, Larry, Roger and I went out for dinner at a very nice steak house. It was there I learned three things about Larry.

First, he did not drink. He was an admitted alcoholic but had been sober for many many years. He did not, however, object to anyone else having a drink.

Second, he had been a pilot for many years but no longer had a desire to fly as a pilot himself.

Third, he was quiet. One never knew what he was thinking. He must have been a great poker player.

We dropped him back at his hotel and agreed I would pick him up at 7am and head to Guthrie, about thirty minutes north of Oklahoma City.

It was an overcast day with rain showers forecast all across the eastern part of the state, but not a serious impediment to flight.

Our first stop was at Broken Bow. I had told Larry this was an early follow-up as the president was a director at another bank that was in final work to complete a director retirement plan.

He had learned about the plan at that bank's board meeting and had asked me to come to his bank to propose a similar plan for his directors. This was my second call with him.

My presentation went very well and Larry had no comments about it.

The next stop was also a second call at a family owned bank in Idabel and the president was so-so on my ideas.

On the way back to Guthrie, after dodging several rain showers, Larry told me he thought I should have done a medical close on the banker in Idabel. That is a traditional insurance agent ploy to motivate a prospect to find out if he or she is even qualified to buy insurance. I had heard of it but told Larry I didn't think that applied to my process for a group plan in a bank.

We returned to his hotel and talked some more and again he mentioned all of the proposals I had been doing. He seemed truly concerned that his office was doing two to three times the booklets for me as they had in the past for other agents.

He was concerned that I was using so many of the covers which were embossed with a gold-plated logo that cost a lot. He said they may have to start charging me for them, and sure enough a bill arrived for covers in a few weeks. When that bill arrived, Roger threw a fit.

Larry had an early flight back and when I dropped him at the airport I simply said that he needed to get ready for the business to begin to flow – and over the coming months it became a river.

Following are stories of banks that became my clients in my first year as my learning curve in bank sales developed.

First board meeting

My first board meeting was in January, 1989, at the very first bank I had called on in El Reno.

I had gone over the proposal with the president and he had arranged a meeting in with one of his directors, a lawyer, at this director's law office

After he had given me a nearly two hour grilling on all aspects of the plan, and I had provided sample legal agreements to him, he finally agreed it appeared to be a plan his bank should do.

I gave a great board meeting presentation after which the president said he would call me the next day. Unfortunately, when he called, he also informed me that after my presentation the lawyer said he had a very good friend who was an insurance agent and wanted him to make a presentation too.

I was a bit upset, called Larry, and Larry gave me lots of talking points and issues to get ready to bring back to the bank.

The long and short of this was that the agent was given my plan presentation, and then adapted it to a proposal system from his insurance company. Fortunately, the president called me and I asked me to come review the other agent's proposal.

This agent presented his proposal at the bank's February board meeting after which the board approved the directors' retirement plan subject to choosing who would be the selling agent.

I took the other agent's proposal and pointed out that he had some significant differences with what we (i.e. my company) understood to be bank accounting guidelines and FDIC rules and regulations.

Most of all, his proposal relied on the future death of the directors to recoup the costs while our program used cost offset accounting based on the interest earnings inside our special high-cash value policies.

I was asked to meet with the lawyer on the board again and came to his office well prepared for my day in court. I did not cast any dispersion on my competition, and, after almost three hours, the lawyer said it became pretty clear that our company was the better choice.

I returned to the board in March and made a second presentation with a handout of the major items for their consideration of how to select a vendor (we were called vendors in the official FDIC regulations) without once saying one thing about my competitor.

I am told he then made a shorter presentation and conceded that it was most likely in the best interest of the bank to select our company.

> NOTE: After the plan was finalized and installed in the bank in August, my competitor called me and asked if there was a job for him with us. I met him and we hit it off and he joined our team in November.

I learned a great deal from this first bank and over time came to know that there was always an insurance agent who had a friend on nearly every board of directors. I learned to take it head-on and only two times in over twenty-years lost to a local agent.

And in one case, after the regulators tore it apart during a bank examination, I was called by the bank to come fix it and take over administration to their plan. The bank then added our life insurance while freezing the competitor's annual premium insurance to reduced paid-up policies with no more premiums.

Learning to understand who is in charge part 1

This is almost funny. I had arranged a meeting with a bank president in January, 1989, who had read my article on director retirement plans and had called me for this meeting.

I had created a sample plan to show him and was deep into my presentation with him when another man entered his office and sat down off to the side.

I continued my presentation focusing upon the president although the other man asked several questions.

After the presentation, the other man left while I remained with the president to set up another meeting with him. I proposed to him that I use real data on all of the bank's directors for a full illustration of this type of plan.

He liked that and after he handed me a census, I asked to review each director for a little background. I noticed that three of them had the same last name, and suddenly it hit me.

I asked who the man was that entered the office while I was doing my presentation to him, and he said, "Oh, he's the owner. He and his mother own all of the stock."

Hmmm. I quickly learned where to focus my attention at all future meetings. Know who you are dealing with and never assume anything just by a title.

This bank became my very first client to fund the plan on April 28, 1989.

Learning to understand who is in charge part 2

This is more of a humorous story similar to the previous one.

Again, I had worked with the president of the bank, but over the course of several meetings I quickly learned this was a 100% owned family bank. One of the owner's two sons worked in the bank and the other was a lawyer whose office was in the bank's building.

I had met with both sons and after getting the plan just the way they thought it should be, they said I would now have to present the plan to their father.

I looked forward to the meeting and as father listened to my presentation with both sons and the president in his office he asked some pretty hard questions.

Finally he said he would approve the plan and I said, "Great. When would you like me to present it to your board of directors?"

"Son," he replied, "you just had a board meeting."

Directors need care too

Nothing can be done of any significance in a bank, especially buying life insurance and approving contracts, without the approval of the board of directors.

Many a non-owner president wanted our plans and helped get it done, but those pesky directors could be really difficult at times.

On one occasion, I had a director vehemently oppose buying (we say funding) the life insurance (remember these were single-premium fully paid-up policies).

He was in his late seventies and he went on and on saying insurance companies were always going broke. I finally asked him if he had any life insurance, expecting his answer to be, "No."

Quite the contrary he proudly said, "Of course I do."

Slightly taken aback for a moment, I then tactfully asked him who he had his life insurance with and he named two well known national carriers.

I said, "Sir, those carriers are the same ones that I am proposing for your bank. Do you believe if they go broke the bank will lose its investment but you would not lose yours?"

He gave me an inquisitive stare and then sat back into his chair saying, "I have no more objections. Let's do this plan."

On another occasion, I worked with another bank and they required a unanimous vote to do just about anything; and they had six directors.

The bank had been 100% owned by two brothers. One had died ten years before and his two children each owned one-fourth.

The other brother, their uncle, was chairman and owned the other half. His one son worked in the bank and he had a daughter outside the bank. His son and the president were the officers proposed for this plan, a supplemental retirement plan.

Unfortunately, he did not understand this program at all and along with his son and daughter had voted no every time. The president and the deceased brother's two children voted yes every time. This stalemate continued for two meetings.

Then the outside nephew held a meeting at his home and asked his two cousins to attend along with me.

I won them over once I found out the issue was the son in the bank had been very jealous of the president who was not family. So his cousin broke through by proposing that they each get the exact same benefit. That appeased the son and his sister.

I re-ran the proposal, went to the next board meeting expecting approval, but was told the next day that the vote was 5 in favor, 1 opposed. The chairman had still voted no.

I was asked to return the next week and meet with him alone. He had a total lack of understanding of the accounting, wondered why the bank had to spend so much money on insurance, and why the bank just couldn't pay the money to the two officers later.

I explained it as simply as possible, when suddenly, he got an expression on his face and said, "Oh, I think I understand it now. We give your company several million dollars to hold and then when my son retires you pay him the benefit."

I replied, "Yes sir."

This was absolutely not how it worked, but I decided that since the rest of the directors understood, and the bank accountant understood, and the end result was the same, agreeing with him was the path of least resistance on my part.

And of course, I also realized that he would most likely be deceased long before anything would ever happen regarding the plan, which became true nine years later.

You can take the boy out of the country, but you can't take the country out of the boy

That's an old saying generally attributed to an article in the May 16, 1914, edition of The Country Gentleman. It is in common usage today including several country and western songs and even once in a movie with Jimmy Stewart.

If you recall the bank I went to in Cherokee on the president's birthday February 14, 1989, and my story about seeing the planes at Enid while driving to it, this event occurred later that summer in July after the board of directors of that bank had approved the director retirement plan I had proposed to them.

A director retirement plan was based on each director signing an agreement to voluntarily defer some or all of his fees to a future date at a very nice interest rate (usually the return on equity of the bank).On that future date the account would be amortized into a monthly retirement benefit.

During the deferral period, if the director died, the life insurance would fund his deferral account to 100% and then pay the planned monthly benefit to his beneficiary immediately. As I slowly learned, many directors in the far-flung rural banks had little or no life insurance – they only had the pine box retirement plan.

On this fine sunny July day I had made appointments with several of the directors at the bank to complete their individual applications; but one director had not made his decision and asked me to meet him at his business – the local sale barn.

I grew up on a corn and cattle farm in rural Nebraska and was not unfamiliar with sale barns. I walked in and he was standing in the central area by the lunch counter (sale barns always had a lunch counter with glass cases that would be filled with pie).

He was dressed as a working cowboy wearing a big Stetson hat, boots (with a mud on them), a brown leather vest over his shirt, and well-worn Levis.

I was in a dark pin-stripe suit, white shirt, colorful tie, and shiny black oxfords. Standing together we probably made quite a sight.

I remarked to him how much I enjoyed going as a youth with my father to sale barns. I ran my hand along the glass pie case and remarked how the homemade pies at the lunch counter always seemed to taste better than my mothers, and the hamburgers were always just a bit more tender and juicy than the local café's.

I asked him to show me the sale arena and we walked out into it together. I stepped carefully in my oxford shoes and survived not stepping in anything too sticky. Finally I suggested we go to his office for him to ask me his questions.

His office was not very big, just a desk with his chair and two across from him, and a long horizontal window in the wall that overlooked the holding pens, all empty today.

We both sat and stared out for several minutes, and then I sighed saying how I had traveled to over fifty countries, but sitting here brought back so many good memories of my youth growing up on a farm.

He turned, looked at me and simply said, "If I do this at the bank and I die, my wife will get all of that money. Is that right?"

I said, "Yes sir, so long as you are healthy and pass a medical exam for the life insurance policy the bank will own on you."

He then looked out the window again and in a quiet even voice said, "I have never had a life insurance policy. I guess I just never gave it any thought. But I want to do this with the bank."

Turning back to me he then said, "So all I need to do is sign up with you today?"

<u>Lessons learned</u>

1. Be prepared. Work hard on your presentations. Be polite but firm – non illegitimi carborundum.

I have always gone into a meeting with the knowledge that I am the smartest person in the room on my topic. No one can best me. Some of the people to whom I am presenting may think I am speaking in Greek. But I accept it, am patient, and never consider anyone's question as out of order.

2. There are rational and irrational objections. The rational ones are easier as they indicate lack of understanding. The irrational ones are harder if you are unable to ascertain where that person is coming from. I eventually loved irrational ones because half the time I could turn them into a humorous story that occurred at another board meeting.

The *single best method* to handle nearly every objection I have ever known is: Feel, Felt, Found.

It goes like this, "Mr. Prospect, I understand how you feel, and many other prospects have felt just like you. After digging into the facts (or further examining the data, etc.), what they found is xxxxx yyyyy is truly the best solution to this problem, etc."

First, you have acknowledged that he has feelings and you are showing him you heard him and have empathy.

Second, you relate that he is not alone. He feels better now knowing that his objection/concern/issue is normal as others have had similar concerns or questions.

Third, you put him in a safety zone with others who found what you are selling became a solution to their problems.

> "People don't ask for facts in making up their minds.
> They would rather have one good, soul-satisfying
> emotion than a dozen facts.
>
> - Robert Keith Leavit

Feel, Felt, Found. Don't leave home without it

3. Always know that many times the key decision maker is not in your audience during early presentations. Be very astute to that especially in corporate selling. The one who actually decides may never meet you, or do so late in the selling process. You need to know who that person or group (committee) is.

4. If it can't be explained in terms that the listener understands, your sale won't get done. Don't lie; but a characterization into another set of terms that results in the same outcome may work better than hours of trying to educate someone on complex accounting or technical concepts.

For example, bank owned life insurance premiums are carried as a bank asset – they are not expensed. I once had a director who could not understand that. To him premiums were expenses.

I always had the background of each director given to me by the president before any board meeting so I could address them by name and personalize my response to each director's question. In this case the director was the local Chevrolet dealer.

Knowing that I then said, "Mr. Chevrolet, if it were possible for you to pay me for your dealership's insurance with a car, and I accepted that, but then said you could keep that car on your showroom floor, you just couldn't sell it, how would you handle that accounting?"

He pondered that a moment and then said, "I think I get it. The bank gives you the cash, and you give us a document saying we still have it at the bank earning interest. Is that right?"

"Yes," I said. And that ended that.

And on another occasion I did the same with a director who was a rancher by using cattle as my example.

(Might make a very messy vault though.)

5. Never ever expect that you will not have competition. Insurance agents lurk behind every rock and nearly everyone has a friend or relative in the business.

(Just kidding.)

To survive competition you must differentiate yourself and your product or service. Remember the shoemaker's sign that read, "Price, Quality, Service – pick any two."

That is the dilemma we all face in sales – how can we do all three?

If you are selling a commodity where price is generally the same, then quality and service are your key sales attributes. Many salesmen think that if they have a price advantage they will always win. The shoe industry has gone that way; but I don't buy cheap shoes as I often stand in them for hours at a time. I seek quality over price.

Does your prospect want the cheapest product? If so you must promote endurance (aka quality) for yours to outlast your competitions.

As an alternative, suggest your prospect could actually be paying more per unit of use (economists call these "utils") if your competitors less costly product needs more frequent repair or simply wears out sooner, thus becoming a higher unit cost for your prospect organization's use.

The salesman's dilemma is always about Price, Quality, or Service. One of those three has to give. Or does it?

So how about this. How about providing your prospect all three by selling at a fair price (probably not the lowest) with the quality level that will do the job (not gold plated). Then always provide the highest possible service, better than your competition, from you and your company (over which you have control).

Generally, I had no control over premium. But if premium was the sole issue, I could use a term product alone, or add a term rider to a smaller universal policy to reduce the required premium. I never made my commission an issue.

Solve the problem for the client. That's how you sell life insurance or anything else.

"Unless you can demonstrate your benefits, all you are left to compete with is price."

- Jeffrey Fry

"Quality is never an accident. It is always the result of intelligent effort."

- John Ruskin

"Being on par in terms of price and quality only gets you into the game. Service wins the game."

- Tony Allesandra

"You'll never have a product or price advantage again. They can be easily duplicated, but a strong customer service culture can't be copied."

- Jerry Fritz

Chapter 10
Would you like fries with your burger?

In January, 1989, after talking with some of the other sales representatives in our agency, I decided to take the Dale Carnegie sales course. I felt it might help me with objections.

In a nutshell, I quickly learned sales tips for selling cameras, or any other product with a point-of-sale strategy. This is taught through the use of a key phrase, "If there were a way you could xxxxx, yyyyy, Mr. Prospect, you would want to know about it wouldn't you?"

This is clearly a loaded question designed to elicit some form of positive reply from the prospect (and it does 99% of the time).

After your prospects response you continue with, "Well, Mr. Prospect, there may be a way you can xxxxx, yyyyy. Let's look at some facts."

I was not initially impressed with these canned phrases. I considered them a form of sales trickery. Duh!

The next thing I learned was how to handle objections. This I liked. I learned how to cushion an objection, rephrase it from a negative into a positive, and to ignore irrational ones.

In the documentary, The Fog of War, Robert McNamara states that when queried by the press, one in power should "...never answer the question being asked of you; answer the question you wish had been asked of you."

I certainly wish I had seen that documentary long before I did, because learning how to rephrase an objection in the Carnegie course into a question for which I had an answer was an immense help for me.

And over the coming years the phrase, "Mr. Banker, if there were a way you could xxxxx,yyyyy…" even crept into my lexicon. With time I reached a point where there was nothing under the sun that I had not heard as an objection – and couldn't answer.

A new horizon

By August, 1989, I had placed $4.8M of single premium life insurance and had another $5M in work. Larry Hendrickson was astounded. He had never had a new guy achieve such a level. In fact, by December only one other agent was ahead of me in total production.

I also hired Harry Dupree, my competitor at the first bank I ever called upon in El Reno, and he began working the state of Oklahoma in December. I began working in Texas and four other states as the agent who had moved from Idaho to Texas two years before to work Larry's program decided to return to Idaho.

As a result, beginning in 1990, I had six states as my territory and found myself running faster than ever before.

Production became such a happening that I actually believed that we would run out of banks to buy into this program in 2-3 years. What a joke that was. It is still being sold to the hard-heads from time to time today.

Winning a case by attacking

I worked with a finder in Mississippi beginning in 1990 until 1995. His name was Sam Fryant and his wife worked for the bankers association. As a result, over the years, he met and knew every bank CEO in the state.

Mississippi was an interesting state. It had always had branch banking so there were only about 95 total banks and the average bank was $250M or more in deposits. And the CEO's were as polite as a $60M bank in rural Oklahoma.

On one of my trips with Sam he had obtained an appointment with a very large bank, just under $1B. We met with the CEO and after a very polite visit he expressed an interest in our program and told us that the CFO would most likely be the primary decision maker. He called the CFO and asked him to see us right then.

We left the CEO's office and went down a couple of floors to the CFO's office. After a short outline of our program, the CFO said he had no use for our ideas. He was not interested in single-premium life insurance saying he thought it was not a proper bank investment.

But, since the CEO had sent us to him, he agreed to give us some data and agreed to a future appointment where his chief investment officer could sit in for our presentation.

We returned several weeks later for out next appointment and were escorted into the main board room. This room had a beautiful wood table about 25 feet long and 10 feet wide with a highly polished surface. We were told to sit in the middle of one side

In about five minutes the CFO and his investment officer entered through a door in the opposite wall and took two seats directly across from us.

There was no chit-chat, the CFO simply asked us to get right down to our proposal. Sam had to get up and carry two copies around the end of the table to them as it was so wide, and then I proceeded to go page by page.

After about ten minutes, the CFO said he clearly understood it, but he could not in good faith accept the risk of an insurance carrier holding the bank's cash and making all investment decisions.

I asked how he measured risk and he said they used Moody's and S&P as the primary means, and consultations with their outside broker dealer to assess their investment holdings.

I pointed out that our insurance carriers were all rated double A or higher by Moody's and by S&P, and asked if he considered that inadequate.

He then stated that the bank had recently written off $125M in guaranteed investment contracts with a life insurance company.

I asked him who that company was and he replied, "Executive Life."

I slapped my hand down hard on the table (recall I did that in Las Vegas once) and then pointed my finger at him and fired my response all the way across ten feet of polished mahogany, "You didn't do your due diligence, did you?"

He was taken aback for a moment, but then replied in a very defensive voice, "Yes we did. They were rated triple A with S&P and Moody's."

I shot back, "You clearly didn't read the portfolio holdings of Executive Life."

"What do mean by read their portfolio?" he fired back.

I turned that question into a question, "Did you know they held junk bonds?"

"No," he replied. "We liked their high yield and their ratings met our criteria for a bond."

I then firmly stated that cash value of an insurance carrier is not a bond, and that before Executive Life failed it was downgraded several times before it reached junk status.

I further stated that Executive Life was well known for offering above market interest rates. When the junk bond market collapsed policy holders lost a lot of their cash value and banks that held guaranteed investment contracts lost all of their equity in them.

At this point the tension in the air of that boardroom was so thick it could be cut with a knife.

I lowered my voice, softened my tone, something I had learned to do in speech training, and continued, "At our company, we provide our bankers a clear analysis of the insurance carriers' investment portfolios, up to and including every bond they hold."

I further went on about how we carefully selected carriers based on their internal guidelines such as no junk bonds, no stocks, and if they had a "fallen angel" bond they were required to sell it.

He replied that his bank had so many bonds or funds that they could not keep up with examining insurance company portfolios.

I then continued by saying that was our job, that we provided a quarterly analysis of each carrier to all our bank clients.

I told him we had even withdrawn sales from a very well-known national life insurance carrier when they significantly changed their portfolio holdings and investment philosophy and replaced all of their policies in our client banks at no cost to the bank and no health requirement for the individual insureds.

Long and short, it was a tough meeting. Sam and I left feeling that perhaps I had overdone it and we probably had little chance of doing business with this bank.

A week later, Sam received a call from the CFO that they wanted another presentation to include portfolio reviews of our carriers and to bring enough documentation that they could send it to their accounting firm.

We did as asked, and in three months Sam and I had the second largest sale in my company's program to date.

Sam was told by the bank's president and CEO that the reason the CFO decided to use our program was based on my zeal and fortitude to stand up to him at that tough meeting.

Over the years the CFO became a regular referral for me and I enjoyed his company at several Mississippi banking conventions.

Once again, you sometimes have to stand your ground, even at the risk of losing a customer. Always be true to thine own self.

Winning a case by withdrawing

There is a very aggressive sales technique known as the takeaway close. I rarely used it but when I did it was powerful.

My partners in Texas had developed a supplemental retirement plan for a bank that had a president who was sixty-two. He owned one-third of the stock and the majority owner was an outside wealthy businessman who owned the rest.

Supplemental retirement plans work like defined benefits plans and require an accrual expense for each participant from the date of the plan to the plan's retirement age. Obviously, the age of each participant drives that cost.

It was rare to have someone over sixty in these plans unless it was the only solution to retire an older family stockholder in order to pass leadership of the bank to the next generation.

I had been brought in on this case by my partners as they were having a very difficult time explaining the accounting. They had previously met with the chairman and knew he was for the plan as he wanted the president to retire with the extra income and not stay at the bank on salary waiting for a pine box departure.

At our board meeting both my partners, David and Kathy, were in attendance since they had begun the plan; however, I had become the plan expert so I was speaking at this point.

The president, the sixty-two year old, was objecting to the plan's cost and really giving me a hard time. I said the only way to do this plan was to accept the accrual cost until he retired. Then the cost would go way down and the accounting impact would turn positive to the bank.

Again and again he objected, and finally said, "I am sorry. I cannot go along with having this much cost to the bank."

I was frustrated beyond belief and simply said back to him, "Okay, you're out of the plan."

With a big flourish I took a red pen out of my pocket and drew a line across his name in my folder and told everyone to do the same in their folders.

My partner David piped up saying, "Lynn, you can't take him out. He's the president."

I turned to David and said, "If he doesn't want the retirement benefit, he's out. With him out the plan the bank has no significant cost and can provide this to the rest of the officers."

I looked at the chairman and he was quietly laughing. I already knew he was for the plan and was not worried about the financial costs, and at this point probably didn't really care if the president wanted in or out.

I turned back to the president and said, "We will need to re-compute the accounting, but your board can tentatively approve the plan today and leave you out."

"No," blurted the president, "I want to be in the plan."

I wrinkled my brow and looked at him with a frown.

"Are you sure?" I said. I wanted to make him squirm.

"Yes," he said in a low voice, "I want the plan so I can retire."

"Okay," I said. And with another big flourish wrote his name back into my book saying, "You're back in the plan."

I then looked up and said, "Are there any more questions?"

After a moment of silence I looked at the chairman and said, "Do you want to vote with us in attendance or shall I and my team leave you for a moment."

By now the chairman had a great big grin as he said we could stay and he called for an immediate vote.

Slowly the president put his hand up with a look on his face wondering how he had been so totally snookered by me.

Do the right thing. It will gratify some people and astonish the rest."

- Mark Twain

Chapter 11

Another fork in the road

When obstacles arise, you change your direction to reach your goal; you do not change your decision to get there.

- Zig Ziglar

In January, 1993, I married a lady from Dallas, Texas. She had been associated with sales and I had met her at the bankers association a year and half before. She was beautiful and I had fallen madly in love with her. But that was not the fork in the road I had to consider.

Which way?

In the summer of 1992, an organization from Dallas was referred by an association member for an endorsement. I had been selected to be the liaison with this organization which was called the National Institute for Estate Planning (NIEP).

Its product was a service to banks where the bank hosted a seminar for their high-net worth clients. These clients could then engage this company and pay a nominal fee for estate planning, use a local attorney for documentation, and then use the bank's insurance agency, or this company's agents, to provide any needed life insurance.

If any life insurance was sold, the bank received a portion of the commission, either through their agency or from the association's agency (thus my involvement). Regulatory rules were complex at that point in time and bank insurance agencies were not commonplace.

The program was very well received and I was impressed by this company (NIEP). On average one-half of all the estate plans called for life insurance to fund trusts or buy-out agreements, and the client rarely went to an outside agent.

In March, 1993, I had a meeting with the president of a bank in central Texas who was doing an estate plan with this company. He was a very large shareholder.

I had been calling on him for nearly a year working on the bank's acquisition of bank owned life insurance and he called me about his estate plan.

The estate planning company (NIEP) wanted him to buy life insurance from them, but he understood the costs were directly to him. Instead he wanted the bank to provide him with insurance. Could I help him? Would I meet with the estate planner?

Of course I said I would, and then called one of the partners in the estate planning company, David Shuster, and discussed this with him. We agreed to both meet with the banker.

I flew into College Station and David picked me up. On the way to the bank, I made it clear to David that using the bank product was far superior for the banker. And at the bank, the banker agreed.

After we left the bank, David made it clear to me he was not happy that he would lose an insurance sale. I suggested I share some of the revenue with him instead of with the bank; and that sparked a great idea.

It's déjà vu all over again

During the drive back to the airport, David proposed that I move to Texas and join his company. When they (NIEP) worked with a bank owner, whether an officer or director, and recommended using life insurance for funding trusts or buy-out plans, I would become the insurance for the bankers and show them how to use the bank (or holding company) to provide that as a benefit to them. It would save the banker a lot of personal cost.

I told David I had to think about it.

In the interim while I was thinking about it, David tried an end run around me by calling my company's president that I worked with and asking for a contract for himself.

The president said absolutely not, that Lynn High had the exclusive contracts for the states of Texas, Oklahoma, Arkansas, Louisiana, Mississippi and New Mexico as his territory.

I never let David know that I knew what he had tried to do. So when I called him to arrange a meeting with him and his partner, Jim Burmeister, he had no choice but to agree.

I flew to Dallas in May and over three days negotiated a contract to join their company.

My new wife was thrilled at the prospect of moving back to Texas; but I was very concerned about having to discuss this radical change with Roger. After all, Roger had been the one who saved me from Saudi Arabia and put me into this incredible program.

Meeting with Roger

I arranged a meeting with Roger in June and told him what I wanted to do. Needless to say, he was shocked.

I had to confess that the push was coming from Susan, my new wife, for when she divorced in Texas she allowed her seven year old daughter to remain with her father in Dallas. By moving back she would be near her daughter again.

Secondly, I clearly viewed this as a chance to expand my opportunity past being just a salesman. David and Jim had offered me a small amount of stock, and they would appoint me as the president of the estate planning service.

My strength as a public speaker had clearly impressed them and they wanted to dramatically expand their operation into a national presence – to live up to their company's name – the *National* Institute for Estate Planning (italics added for emphasis).

Roger asked for some time to consider all of this. He was more than my boss, he was my friend.

I felt a sense of betrayal on my part; but my new wife had to be my priority and the potential of being part of a growing organization in which I had an ownership stake outweighed my current position in the bankers association's insurance agency.

In a few days Roger and I met again and he agreed to my departure. He asked for no conditions, but I agreed that the state of Oklahoma would become Harry's territory. We also agreed I would remain an employee until December 31, 1993, as my contract had revenue sharing and we both wanted to maximize that revenue for our mutual benefit.

And with that, I began to plan my move to Texas.

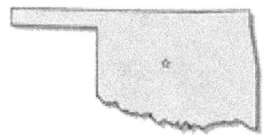

Every new beginning comes from some other beginning's end.

- Seneca

Chapter 12
David Shuster

David Shuster was an idea man, a superb salesman, and had a very powerful personality.

David grew up in West Palm Beach, Florida, where his father was a golf course pro. David learned to play golf at an early age and received a golf scholarship to the University of Houston.

After college he played on the PGA tour four years, winning one tournament. As he openly stated, "I could drive for show, but couldn't put for the dough."

David could make a golf ball do just about anything with a driver. I loved to watch him send one around a tree or right over it and then drop. He could make it stay low into the wind and then run an extra fifty yards on the fairway. He said he even won the long ball drive once during his four years as a pro.

And then one day, during a swing on the fairway, his back went out. The doctors told him he would never play golf again, so he became an insurance agent.

He joined a firm in Florida and sold a deferred directors fee plan to banks and businesses that simply used the fee as the premium and whatever the policy made in cash value became the retirement benefit; but if the director died before he retired the policy paid the face amount to his family.

The National Institute for Estate Planning (NIEP)

David Shuster was bigger than life to me. He was the best salesman I had ever known, full of bravado and energy. When David first met me in 1992 he was fascinated by our special single-premium bank only life insurance.

I was impressed with his company's strategy to get inside a bank. Furthermore, his company was endorsed by several of the independent state bankers association, and was on the verge of gaining the Independent Community Bankers Association of America's endorsement.

Jim Burmeister, the founder, had developed an incredible method of gaining access to high-net worth individuals by using the credibility of those individuals' banking relationships.

All Jim had to do was recruit the bank which was not that difficult as the bank would be compensated on any life insurance sold, and the community would receive an essential service as goodwill to the bank. It was a win-win for everyone.

Jim gave a powerful seminar on estate planning. The estate tax laws were very complex in the 1990's, and the seminar had great appeal. Many banks would host two or even three presentations over a year's time.

The NIEP had about fifteen full time employees and about twenty in-house agents. They placed millions of dollars of annual premium policies and were very profitable. But they lacked a strategy for bank owners, especially when the owner was a director but not an employee.

Bank regulations were very adverse to using bank capital or funds to aid a director. Many banks did not have a holding company and NIEP developed a key relationship with a major law firm in Dallas.

This law firm had a banking division that needed a method of being brought into a bank and we needed them to do the legal documentation for our estate planning clients.

In the process, we would introduce them to banks without a holding company and through us they obtained many new bank clients through our prospecting efforts.

NOTE: Laws and regulations were quite restrictive in the '90's and lawyers were not allowed to go out prospecting for bank clients; thus, by our introduction, they had a new source of clients and we had an ally for our estate planning strategies.

Why is this important? Because if a bank had a holding company, the holding company could make an agreement to buy back a shareholders stock. To do so directly with a bank shareholder was forbidden under banking regulations.

If I may pat myself on my back, I developed a complex forecasting model for future holding company stock values and then fashioned a mirror life insurance policy owned and funded by the holding company using dividends from the bank.

This worked in banks that had two desires:

1. To remain an independent community owned and operated bank; and

2. To provide stockholders who had more of their estate outside of their holding company stock the opportunity to sell that stock back to the holding company with a pre-arranged pricing formula to create cash liquidity inside their future estate upon their death. And they paid nothing for the life insurance held by the bank holding company. A real cost offset for them.

As a result of this idea and my forecasting model, the need for bank owned life insurance, for which I held the contract, became a major source of revenue to NIEP.

Soon we were spreading out to states outside of my six-state contract, and this brought a major issue to my company. Each representative had a contract for specific states and had agreed to not work in another representative's state without permission; and that permission was rarely granted.

Who then would be allowed to make the sale to the bank or holding company outside of my contracted states?

Further, it was becoming obvious that the major national banking association that had endorsed NIEP was not happy with our across the board strategy for bank customers; they wanted us to focus only on banks.

The net result of these two issues was discord; and if there is one thing both bankers and their associations do not want it is discord.

When you come to a fork in the road, take it

This time the fork in the road was not created by me. It was created by the company with whom I held the contract for bank owned life insurance, thus a territory conflict.

And within NIEP David had created a new sister company called the National Institute for Community Banking (NICB), thus an endorsement conflict.

As a result of these issues, David and Jim reached an amicable split and David and I took NICB as our company and Jim took sole ownership of NIEP. This occurred in the fall of 1995.

David and I then provided a share of our stock to two key individuals, Kathy Smith and Kelly Earls, whom we had trained to work on both seminars and bank shareholder estate plans.

We then met with the owner of the company I held my contract with, Larry Hendrickson, and negotiated a method to work in another representative's territory and share the commissions on any sale of bank owned life insurance.

The four of us then began a nationwide seminar program using NICB providing exclusive services to banks.

From small planes to big planes

When I moved to Texas in the fall of 1993, I searched for a flying club and found a small group of pilots who owned a Mooney 231 (a four seat single engine plane). Each person had an equal share and had to pay a fixed hourly rate to fly plus his own fuel.

I started flying to banks at the far reaches of Texas (and that is an understatement) and had great success. But now with our NICB seminar strategy, I also began to fly more than the club allowed.

I sold my share in the Mooney and bought a Piper Aztec in the spring of 1995. Besides, my partner David traveled with me often and David was six feet, four inches tall and weighed 300+ pounds.

Bankers would marvel how David and I could even fit into that plane as I was six feet and 215 pounds. The Aztec made a lot of sense as it was roomy, had two engines and could lift a lot of weight.

Success is a wonderful thing. We had more and more banks engaging us all across the nation and were meeting ourselves coming and going. It was time for more planes.

In 1996 I traded the Aztec for a Piper Malibu and outright bought a Piper Mirage. We hired a full time pilot and we operated coast to coast.

In early 1998 the Malibu crashed one night due to engine failure with only the pilot on board. Thankfully he walked away unhurt but the plane was a total loss.

I then bought a Cessna 310 twin engine as a replacement with the insurance payment as several of our sales employees no longer wanted to fly in a single-engine.

The Mirage was approaching engine overhaul and we were flying further and further so that summer I traded the Cessna and the Mirage for two Piper Cheyenne twin engine turbo-prop aircraft. We were now running a mini-airline operation.

Once again, I was in heaven. I flew my own plane virtually everywhere I went; and I was selling without any cold calling as the seminars, of which I was a principle speaker along with David or Kathy, brought in all of our prospects.

Two more forks in the road

In 1998 the company with whom I held the contract for bank owned life insurance was sold to a national consulting firm called Clark-Bardes. Little changed in our sales, but they instituted a much better arrangement with representatives in other states.

NICB had also grown to 24 employees and we were going strong. We were going so strong, that in May, 1999, after four months of negotiations, Clark Consulting (renamed from Clark-Bardes after going public on the NYSE) elected to buy out NICB.

We then became a division of this consulting company and David and I and our two junior partners received stock in the buying company and five year employment contracts.

During the negotiations Clark Consulting wanted us to give up our airplanes, but after bringing in a summary of three prior months travels, we challenged them to plan how they would have done all that travel through commercial sources only. It only took one day to become readily apparent that our sales would decline about $1 for every $0.50 of savings in travel.

We had created success through our planes because the vast majority of our bank clients were flung all across the nation in small communities and our planes allowed us to conduct almost twice as many meetings as any other means of travel.

David Shuster'isms

I stated earlier that David was the best salesman I had ever known, full of bravado and energy. He was colorful and humorous and it was a treat to travel with him. But David also had a lot of good old fashioned B.S. in him too.

The stories I am about to relate mostly happened prior to 1999 as once we were bought out by Clark Consulting in May of that year we were divided into four sales teams lead by the four prior owners. But whenever David and I did travel together the chemistry was awesome.

What follows are some stories that I call Shuster'isms. I hope you enjoy them and find the sales strategy used in each one as well as the humor.

He's my pilot.
One time David had a board meeting in northern Missouri and I had a board meeting in western Iowa, both on the same day.

David's was at 2pm and mine was at 7pm, so we flew together and planned to spend the night in Iowa.

It was a totally clear day; no flying issues existed. When we landed in Missouri I told David I would just wait at the airport aviation center. But when the banker walked in to greet David and pick him up to go to the bank, David introduced me as his pilot and pointed out our plane.

David held a belief that people liked to do business with successful people and he was a bit of a braggart, always showing off our planes. And making me his pilot was a boost to his ego.

The banker and I exchanged pleasantries and a handshake. I moved to sit down when the banker said to David that I should go along as it would be more comfortable for me at the bank. David agreed and we all three drove away.

Once in the bank, David asked if it was alright for me to sit in on the meeting. The banker said no problem so I took a seat in the far left corner of the room and assumed a disinterested slump.

David was about half way through his presentation when a director asked him a really difficult accounting question. After a moment of silence David called to me to answer so I stood up and did so. The director accepted my answer and I sat back down.

In about five minutes, another director asked another really tough question and David immediately called my name and asked me to provide the answer.

Again, I stood up, gave my answer, received a follow-up question, answered it, and then sat back down.

At this point, the banker who picked us up (he was the chairman of the board) looked at David and said, "I thought you told me he was your pilot. How does he know so much about the accounting for your plan?"

David squirmed for a moment and then admitted that I was his partner and knew all about our plans. One of the other directors laughed and said, "Maybe you should learn to fly and let him do all of the presentations."

David laughed and agreed and then several other directors also laughed as they looked at me.

On the way back to the airport, David apologized to the chairman who laughed it off as the board had approved the plan.

<u>You must be very expensive if you can own that plane</u>

This is one of the most memorable of my Shuster'isms.

David and I had flown together in my Malibu in 1996 to Corsicana, Texas, for a first call on a bank.

On the way, David said this was going to be a tough sale as the banker had not wanted to meet with us at all; however, his chairman had been to our seminar and had made the arrangement.

After landing I parked right in front of the aviation center building and the banker was standing there waiting for us.

As David stepped out and walked over to him with me in trail, the banker loudly said to David, "You guys sure must charge a lot to fly a plane like that."

David said that actually it was more practical as we could visit two or three banks a day and return home without having to spend money on hotels. The banker grunted something without a smile.

We rode to the bank in near silence and had our meeting. The banker was a grumpy one and tried to blow holes in our discussion over and over; but David and I stood our ground with him.

We left the bank (he drove a very new model Mercedes) in silence. About half way to the airport David, who was sitting in the back seat, asked him if he played golf.

He said, 'Yes."

I then turned to him and said that David had been a PGA professional golfer for four years and his response was, and I am not kidding, "What! That big slob played golf as a professional!"

This banker was not long on tact as during our presentation he used quite a bit of profanity. I told him again David had been a PGA player and was the best golfer I had ever seen.

At this point we turned into the airport entrance and I want you to picture this. The entrance road was new concrete two lanes wide and made a perfectly straight line right up to the doors of the aviation center building. The banker drove straight up and parked.

After he stopped, but before he got out of the car, David said, "Hey, do you have your clubs in the car?"

The banker stepped out saying, "Yes I do."

"Get'em out!" David ordered.

They walked to the trunk and the banker pulled out his bag. David reached and pulled out the driver and then put out his other hand to the banker saying, "Give me a ball."

David then turned and said, "Do you see that tree at the end of the entrance road?"

The banker and I both looked and right across the highway, about 150 yards away, stood a single big oak tree with a wide trunk.

David said to the banker, "If I can hit that tree trunk with this ball, will you do business with me?"

The banker laughed and said, "Buddy, if you can hit that tree trunk I will give you my car."

David stepped forward a few feet, put the ball on the bare concrete behind the car, wound up and "Swish!"

That ball flew straight as a bullet and we heard "Whack." Then we saw that white golf ball drop straight down the front of that tree trunk to the ground. The banker and I stared in total disbelief.

Then he blurted out, "You can't have my car."

David said, "Gim'me another ball."

The banker complied and again we heard "Swish" followed by "Whack" and could see the ball fall to the ground again.

At this point the banker grabbed the driver from David's hands, turned it club head bottom up and looked feverously for scratches. There were none.

David said, "When do you want to have the board meeting to approve our proposal?"

The banker mumbled he would call, threw the bag and the club into the trunk, slammed it shut, got in his car and drove away.

At the plane I looked at David and said, "Can you always do that?"

"Yes," he replied.

<u>If it could be true it's not a lie.</u>

David had lots of expressions, but I always liked this one the best, "If it could be true, it's not a lie."

David could exaggerate and stretch the truth further than anyone I ever knew; but he was honest and would never steal a penny. He loved free coupons and money off deals, calling them found money, but honest he was.

When he exaggerated to bankers, making it true fell to me or Kathy to figure out how to do it.

My favorite was a board meeting in central Texas near Brenham. I had not been with David on this assignment but for the final board meeting he had asked me to go with him as the prior board meeting had been very difficult. He said this was our last chance to get the deal.

He told me the president wanted the plan, but had little pull with the directors as he was a "hired gun" and the plan would boost his personal retirement and hopefully retain several of the key loan officers.

But the directors were just not getting how it was paid for by life insurance or why the bank should even give these officers any more money.

At the board meeting, David arranged for me to sit right across from him in the center of a long board room table.

David was doing quite well with his proposal, and then he told a whopper. One of the directors said that was impossible to do, and did so very forcibly.

The director said to David, "Who in the world could possibly do that?"

David pointed at me saying, "He can."

"Who me?"

The director turned to me saying he did not believe it.

I calmly answered that our company could do exactly that. All I had to do was revise a set of software that I had created before and I would have it done for them to review in a week.

Well, as it turned out, the board voted to approve David's plan subject to my doing what David had promised.

"If it could be true, it's not a lie."

(Hmmm. I need to make up some software.)

I made sure it was true; and also made David promise to never do that to me again.

May I vote too

Once at a bank, right in front of David, the board voted on his proposal. The vote was 5-5. Tied.

David asked to make a few more comments and, after doing so, he asked them to vote again.

The president called for the vote and it was 6-5 this time.

Perplexed, the president asked who had not voted the prior time. After he figured out there were only ten directors present, he turned to David and David confessed he voted too.

At that moment, according to David, the board erupted in laughter and the president called for another vote. This time the plan was approved 8-2; and without David's vote.

Pizzazz and hubris; that was David's way.

<u>Guns, bank examiners, and taxi drivers</u>

David's humor had no limit. Sometimes it was a bit sardonic as these three quick examples come to mind.

<u>Guns.</u> One day, after a board meeting, David and I got into a taxi outside the bank to return to a commercial airport and he swung his briefcase into the back seat saying, "Lynn, we couldn't have gotten more money out of that bank with AK-47's."

I laughed so hard I almost came to tears.

<u>Bank examiners.</u> Another time, we landed our plane pretty late in a small Iowa town. We asked the airport aviation service if there was still any place in town open for food.

The only place was a bar called Pinky's. We went straight there and when we walked in it was full of people. We were both in business suits and together we stuck out like two sore thumbs.

The waitress was nice to us and said we had five minutes to order. We did so quickly; and when she returned for a drink order she asked what we were doing in this small town. Clearly, she said, they didn't see guys in pinstripe suits very often.

David said we were bank examiners and were in town to correct some problems with one of the local banks. He said we could not say any more about it. We ate our meal and left for the one motel in town.

In the morning we drove to the bank about ten minutes before nine when it opened, and there were about twenty people gathered at the entrance.

"Oops," said David. "Maybe we better wait and find the back door."

We drove to the back of the bank and waited until after nine before we walked in. When we reached the president he said it was a really odd morning as a large number of people had come in to withdraw their money. Some were saying they had heard the bank was in trouble.

Taxi drivers. On another occasion, we flew into San Antonio and had an appointment with a bank we had both been before.

It was a large building and they had a back entrance, so we asked the taxi driver to pull up to it. We gave him enough cash to cover the meter, but David told the driver that we needed him to wait for us as we would only be in the bank a few minutes.

David further told the driver to keep the motor running and be ready to leave quickly when we did come out.

At one minute to nine, we got out holding only our briefcases and wearing sunglasses. We stood at the door until a person came and opened it and then darted right in.

We stopped in the shadows for a moment and sure enough, that driver hit the gas and raced away. I am sure he thought we were going to rob the bank and use him as our getaway.

If it's worth doing, it's worth overdoing.

This was a classic Shuster'ism. It certainly applied to eating as he would order the breakfast special plus a second full side plate. No wonder he weighed 325lbs.

But when he was in his selling mode, he simply kept going and going until the banker had no choice but to surrender.

His ability to say the right things plus his physical appearance may have been overwhelming to many bankers.

This saying has stuck with me over time as I took it to mean persistence, as David clearly had that.

<u>Silence? Never heard of it.</u>

This is my last Shuster'ism because it amplifies one of my selling tactics – but not David's.

I learned many years before that when you have asked your prospect a key question, one you know he has to answer, the best way to continue is to keep your mouth shut until he does.

I have waited over a minute in many cases and even had a few prospects break out in a visible sweat; but in the end the old adage that the first to speak loses is true.

By waiting out the answer, 9 times out of 10, the prospect will reveal their true objection; or if they had a key misunderstanding.

Now, for this story, put yourself in the conference room at the Waco, Texas, commercial airport.

David and I had flown in to meet with a banker who owned majority control of his bank. David had completed his estate plan and he clearly needed to pursue the final recommendation to use life insurance. But he was hesitant and had made a number of weak excuses in several prior meetings with us.

He agreed to drive into Waco and meet us in the airport's conference room as his small nearby town had no airport. The conference room had a V-shaped table with swivel chairs on wheels along each of the extended sides.

David took the one chair at the head of the table, the banker was on David's left, and I was on David's right, across from the banker. There was one empty chair between David and each of us.

After about fifteen minutes of bantering back and forth, David posed a key question that put the banker on the spot.

The banker looked at me and I shrugged my shoulders with a nod of my head. In about ten seconds I saw the banker take a depth breath, and I was sure he was going to speak, when David suddenly answered the question for him.

The banker then smiled and laughed. He knew he was off the hook.

I took my left foot and pushed the empty chair across the open space towards David saying, "You need to know when to keep quiet."

The banker stood up saying, "I have to leave. I need to get back to the bank. I will give you guys a call in a few days."

I cursed David all the way back to our plane.

In about three weeks, I drove to the banker's hometown and dropped in on him unannounced.

We both laughed about that last meeting in Waco, but when I posed the same question to him he looked at me saying, "You aren't going to let me off the hook this time, are you?"

I shook my head side to side and remained silent. He simply looked at me at me in defeat and said, "Okay, let's do the deal."

Lessons learned.

The most important thing I learned from David was to always be in charge. From my years in the air force I knew that projecting a poised and confident posture to your prospect was important.

I just had a hard time with some of David's pranks, but I can say he kept me on my toes and made me stretch and grow.

Here is what he taught me:

1. Never give up.

2. You are always the smartest person in the room on whatever you are trying to say and do on your program.

3. You have teammates in your office staff to help you make things happen. Call on them when needed.

4. Trust your gut. You know when a prospect is giving you a B.S. reply. Learn how to use that against them later to turn your sale around.

5. Have fun. Life is too short not to have fun. Humor will relieve you of many of your offences in life.

And now, one last really great story.

Actors all

David and I would rehearse every meeting before we entered the bank. And I trained all of my protégés to do the same.

Every meeting had three requirements/conditions.

First, review what you had discussed to date and have firm agreement on progress made up to this meeting.

Second, state up front the time you plan to take for this meeting; then get agreement from your prospect and stick to it. They can ask you to run over; but you should never ask for more time. If you do you have not prepared adequately or made your case.

Third, know what you want for an outcome. Most of the early meetings in our sales process had the sole outcome of being invited back for another meeting.

Why these three goals? Because ours was a complex sale, one that most bankers didn't really understand as it was not standard banking and required accounting concepts that many bankers had never seen or heard of before.

Each of the early meetings, and follow-on meetings with new players (a key director, CPA or attorney), always had to push forward the knowledge the banker needed to make a decision – even if he had no idea what that knowledge was.

The following story is about a first call on a fairly large bank in central Texas near Austin. The president had called David after reading an article I had written in an association magazine.

The bank president told David they wanted to know about how to do a supplemental retirement plan because their bank had just begun a new defined contribution plan and senior officers like him, with many years of prior service, could not get a full retirement in the years they had remaining.

Further, he told David, he did not want a presentation on bank owned life insurance. That had been presented before by some other company and he did not like that idea. He asked David to please just provide them with the rules that applied to a supplemental retirement plan and what it would cost.

David and I discussed this on the flight down through our headsets and decided David would open the meeting and introduce me as the company's expert on supplemental retirement plans.

I would describe how they worked, all of the accounting, and outline benefits versus cost. I had prepared some generic examples so this plan sounded good.

David had already told me all about the president's saying not to discuss bank owned life insurance, but we decided that when I had finished my accounting discussion I would then say something like, "And now, of course, you will want to fund this with bank owned life insurance to eliminate the cost."

David would then jump in abruptly and loudly say to me, "Oh Lynn, I forgot to tell you. They don't want to use any insurance to offset plan costs. Don't talk about that."

That was our plan – two actors going through a planned script.

And sure enough, the president, who had the chairman sitting in his office for this presentation too, said, "Oh no. If that's important and can eliminate the cost, we should know about that."

The chairman nodded saying, "Of course we should know all of our options."

And as they say, the rest is history. We sold one very large case because David and I were good actors with well-prepared lines.

I shared this story some years later with the president and he laughed and laughed saying he deserved it.

David once said I was the greatest actor he had ever known. I could be taking a nap, be awakened and asked to give a fifteen minute speech, just flip a switch inside me and begin, "Ladies and gentlemen. We are here today to blah, blah, blah."

Chapter 13

And then there were three

At approximately 8 o'clock on the evening of October 10, 2000, my associate Kathy Smith called me at my home.

Her voice was trembling as she told me that my friend and partner, David Shuster, had been killed in a plane crash in southern Texas that afternoon.

I sat down in disbelief and began to weep. Kathy sobbed as she told me a little more about what was known at that point. Then we hung up.

David Shuster was bigger than life to me. He was my friend and mentor in sales and I loved that man.

As time went by we recovered and went back to work, but I think about him often and wonder what our company and my life would have been had he lived.

I miss him and will always remember his Shuster'isms.

Over the years since his death, when I was in a difficult sales situation, I would just ask myself, "What would David do?"

And then I'd do it.

<u>About the plane crash.</u>

First, it was not one of my two planes. Both of them were scheduled out that day so David had contracted a rental plane and pilot at the local airport.

Second, the full story of what happened will never be known. David was killed outright and the pilot suffered severe head injuries and remained in a coma for years. Even today, as far as I know, he is still mentally unfit from his head injuries to say what happened.

What is known is that the plane ran out of fuel (it was a twin engine). The airport used for the meeting did not have fuel and a follow-on flight was scheduled to another airport to obtain fuel after the meeting.

It had taken longer to fly to the original airport due to weather; and on the next flight the plane crashed about five miles short of the intended airport. And that is all anyone knows.

Chapter 14

What I have learned about sales and life

Flexibility is the key to making life work and being enjoyable. If you don't enjoy what you do, your life is just a boring journey to the cemetery.

<u>What is the difference between a fork in the road and a crossroad?</u>

When you come to a crossroad, you have three options. One is to keep going straight. The other two choices are a turn to the right or a turn to the left. Those two turns go in opposite directions.

The last choice in my sales career was a crossroad; and I turned left. I left my established company at the end of my employment contract in 2004 and went with my two remaining partners to start over again – and it didn't work out.

Soon I was at another crossroad; and once again I turned. I left my two former partners in 2005 and struck out on my own with a company that had always been a prime competitor.

<u>Final chapter in my sales career</u>

It was tough being a lone ranger again, and at an age where I knew it was for the last time.

My new company was called Benmark and they hired me to assist them on joint sales projects with their agents. They needed a strong sales representative to get their hard-headed banker prospects to buy their product (still bank owned life insurance).

I also began training selected agents on a new program involving compensation reviews and incentive payment plans. This had become a major issue in banking at this time and hiring loan officers was a highly competitive arena. I teamed up with an outside fee-based consultant named Jack Watson.

Then, in 2007, Benmark was sold to a new organization called Renaissance Bank Advisors and at the same time a new accounting pronouncement from the Financial Accounting Standards Board (FASB) occurred that required a serious revision to a plan that Benmark had offered over many years before.

I was retained on a two year contract to lead a small team to fix the problem caused by this new accounting regulation.

Basically, the former Benmark had created a supplemental retirement plan on which the future benefit was based upon how well the life insurance policy performed versus a specific bank earnings index.

Thus it was called the Indexed Retirement Plan and had not required any cost accounting on the bank's financial statement other than a current liability. It did not account for the future value of the benefit expense until this new pronouncement by the FASB.

As a result of the new FASB ruling, banks either had to expense a rather large catch-up accrual (an immediate charge to earnings); or cancel the plan. Since the plans had never had vesting, it became a serious issue with the officers who were in the plans.

All in all it was a most controversial project for about 185 banks in the eastern half of the nation that had this plan and I was the lead representative to go to each bank and fix it.

Thank goodness I was not the one who ever sold it, and as a result I was successful in amending the plan in about 75% of the banks who had it. The remaining 25% of banks simply cancelled it.

But the most fun thing I did for those two years when I remained with the new company was traveling all across the eastern part of the country seeing places I had never been.

I had an apartment in Atlanta, Georgia, our headquarters, and one in Winston-Salem, North Carolina, all while keeping my home in Dallas, Texas.

I loved it.

Lessons learned

Life without challenge is boring.

I feel sorry for people who have never had to depend on living by their wits. I don't mean being a grafter; I mean someone who simply followed the rules and did his or her job, came home every day, and watched the news and sports without every actually being a part of it.

My mind never stops thinking about a better way to do something, and that is what makes a great salesman. And I also learned from dealing with other great salesmen.

A great salesman is always thinking about the next step for his or her client – 24/7. Now that is not a boring life.

If you want certainty, settle for a salary.

I had certainty in the air force. I had a paycheck deposited every month like clockwork. Hmmm. I guess it was clockwork.

I was not without challenge in the air force, as I flew hard and survived 440 combat missions with only one bullet's dent in my chest; but my issue throughout my military service was that I could work 40 hours a week or 70 hours a week but my payroll deposit was always the same.

As a pilot or staff officer, I truly did work 70 hours a week and on some occasions 80-90 hours a week when I was on deployments. And that was a grind.

I often heard the non-flyers complain at the bar how the flyers were always treated better and promoted better, which in fact we were, but we worked harder and longer and at constant risk to our lives.

My point is that statistics and surveys show that to get ahead in your chosen career, you have to do just that. You have to work harder and longer than the other folks.

So ask yourself if you want a home life or career success. No matter what the talking heads say on TV or opinion editors in the papers, there is no balance making it equal.

The scale has to tip to one side or the other – and that choice is yours.

<u>Life is unpredictable, especially if you are in sales.</u>

You have clearly seen that my life had a lot of forks in my road and in the end two serious crossroads.

I am not unhappy with the outcome. There is an old saying that you are not old until your regrets outnumber your dreams.

I still have dreams. I dream this book will change someone's life and help them achieve their own individual greatness.

I dream that his book will carry my dear friend David's name several more generations beyond his, as I believe a person is not dead so long as one living person remembers him.

In the movie Troy there is a scene where the Greek king is berating Achilles (played by Brad Pitt) saying his name will be carved on statues and will live on – not Achilles name.

But whose name did live on? Everyone remembers Achilles name; who knows the king's.

The greatest challenges salesmen face in their individual lives is the unpredictable nature of their income and their own self-doubt. Does the latter perhaps cause the former?

Perhaps, but I believe I could sell matches in hell; I just don't like making the phone call for an appointment with the devil.

> "Make the most of your regrets; never smother your sorrow, but tend and cherish it till it comes to have a separate and integral interest. To regret deeply is to live afresh."
>
> > - Henry David Thoreau

> "There are no regrets in life, just lessons."
>
> > - Jennifer Aniston

If you can figure out the difference in these two quotes, one from over 150 years ago, one from current times, and apply them equally you will succeed.

Chapter 15

Team selling

This chapter is a stand-alone treatise on team selling of a singularly large product. Such products will always involve a sales process, not just a, "If there were a way you could xxxxx, you'd want to know about it wouldn't you?" point-of-sale strategy.

Basically it is the strategy I developed when I was given an expanded territory began working with other agents, both as finders and as partners.

I gained immense experience working with banks from as little as $50M in footings to as much as $5B in footings; and from a single one-time $50K single-premium key man policy to a $100M single-premium investment only sale.

And guess which one was the hardest? Yes, the $50K in a little bank. The big bank already wanted the product; we just had to compete on price and service.

I also read voraciously about sales. I once heard a speaker at a sales convention state, "If you read novels in your spare time, you are either spending too much time not working or you are a lousy salesman. Only read biographies of the great salesman and books on how to improve your sales skills."

The speaker also applied this to non-sales professions; and I agree. If you want to excel at sales you have to think it all the time. You are never so good you cannot improve. After all, the room for improvement is the largest room in the world.

Three secrets of team selling

The most incredible part of being on a sales team is division of labor. This does now mean that you have only one talent; it means that you have a specific role to play on that sale.

I often subjugated my role to my finder/team associate even though I could do any and all of the roles if needed. I would let them put me on a pedestal as a subject matter expert so I could drill into the facts, even being pushy about them, and let the finder/team associate push for the sale.

Secret number one

When you are on a sales call alone, who is watching you and monitoring what you say?

The first secret of team selling is that when one of the team members is talking, the other team member is listening – and watching.

Ever notice that when someone is under stress they act differently?

Every notice your prospect thumbing through your proposal booklet to some future page while you are trying to explain the data on the current page?

Every notice your prospect looking at his watch; or at the clock on the wall; or doodling on the pages of your proposal?

If you don't notice that because you are so focused on what you are saying, you will almost always lose that sale.

When working as a team, your second team member is the one to listen and watch and when he or she notices these "tells" begin to occur, he or she should jump in.

I would jump in like this to my associate who was making the presentation when I saw the prospect wandering away:

Me: "Just a minute associate, you just said blah, blah, blah. I am confused. Does that mean blank blank or blink blink?"

Associate: "Oh. Well Lynn, it means blank blank and because of that bing bing will happen?

Me: "Mr. Prospect, is that what you heard? Is bing bing what you want?"

And with that the sales presentation is back on track and the prospect is reengaged.

Now if that happens a lot, then your sales associate needs some more training on presentations, for example, how to do check points with the prospect to ensure they are following what has been said up to that point, or if they have any questions at that point.

Another benefit of team selling is it allows junior associate to learn and expand their skills knowing they will not be allowed to fall down during a meeting. I (or David or Kathy or Kelly), the true team leader, would be there to rescue them and they knew it.

And when that happened, don't hold it against the junior team member, go over it later allowing them to learn and grow. And if they don't you can revise their employment status at a later time.

Secret number two

The biggest difference between a one-person sales activity and a team sales activity is that one team member is working the relationship with the prospect, and the other team member is positioned as a subject matter expert.

For example, in sales of products by engineers, the lead sales representative is always an engineer, but he is now functioning as the prospect manager. He brings in other engineers to be the subject matter experts.

Why? Because he (the lead) can sit beside the prospect and query the other engineer(s) about the science behind the product and ensure that the prospect understands it. This is especially true if the prospect at this point does not fully understand the data or proposition. Let me explain.

Although I was normally the true team sales leader in authority on a team sale, I nearly always become the subject matter expert of the team. I allowed my junior associate to lead the sales call and handle the client relationship.

Why? Because I had heard it all before. I was the most capable on the team and had watched bankers fidget in their chairs, make irrational arguments, or in some other way try and deflect our sales process. Rarely did a banker jump up and say, "I want to buy that now! When can you deliver it?"

NOTE: Remember in chapter 9 at the start of my banking career when Roger divided bankers into three groups? By this point in my career we were deep into the second third and beginning to call on the hard-headed bankers in the final third. The low hanging fruit was gone.

For example, if the lead representative in charge of the relationship is working the meeting and is getting into trouble with the prospect, he or she could then turn to me and say, "Mr. High, have you encountered this issue before with our product?"

By doing this simple transfer, the sales associate puts me on the spot knowing that I know the answer, and the lead associate can now take sides with the prospect on the issue.

For example follow this conversation:

Associate: "Lynn, have you seen this problem before in other banks?"

Me: "Yes I have, and what I found is that bankers do blah, blah, blah."

Associate: "I don't understand that Lynn. How did that change a banker's use of the product?"

Me: "Well, blah, blah, blah."

Associate: "I think I see."

Then the associate turns directly to the prospect and says, "Mr. Prospect, if what Lynn says is true would that solve your concerns of using our product?"

I call this a role reversal. The lead associate has reversed from being the one pushing the sale to the prospect to now becoming a member of the prospects team defending why the sale should even occur. The associate is now opposing me!

I had to train my junior sales associates to do this. It wasn't natural. We role played and rehearsed how to set up this situation so they could become a de facto trusted member of the prospects team and put me, the expert, on the spot. And it worked.

By doing so we were able to elicit whether the prospect simply didn't understand the issue and/or how our solution worked for him. Or we could ferret out the prospect's true objection by siding with the prospect and exploring what they were feeling.

The lead associate could put up touchy-feely objections to me allowing the prospects internal concerns to be addressed even when he was not voicing them.

This method worked so well that after my early years in the bank sales, our company implemented team selling as the only strategy and our group had the highest closing ratios across all of our sister offices.

<u>Secret number three</u>

This is an extreme event but it happens. Sometimes, a sales representative (associate) or a subject matter expert (me) becomes at odds with a prospect. There is a personality dysfunction.

If that occurs, that team member must be replaced. If it is the relationship member, the second member simply takes over. I have had to do that several times for an associate; and the same thing occurred a few times when I was the person that just didn't click with the prospect.

If the issue was with the subject matter expert, that was an easier fix. We had more than enough of them so that if the lead sales representative felt that the prospect wanted a new voice at the table, it was easy to do. Any simple excuse would do.

Sometimes changing a team member allowed a fresh start with a difficult situation or prospect. As I mentioned in the case at the Waco airport, that happened. I went without David to see that prospect and closed the case.

And that is why you want a partner who understands Abraham Lincoln's old saying, "You can please all of the people some of the time, some of the people all of the time, but you can't please all of the people all of the time."

Is it better to secure the sale and hurt someone's ego, including your own; or to forgo the sale?

David and I had an easy answer for that. We didn't care who carried the money home to our bank, we just wanted to be sure one of us had a bag of money to carry!

David once told a bank CEO that if he did the plan, he (David) would never come back to bank. In fact, the banker could just lose his phone number. Of course, he then gave the banker my phone number.

Know when to check your ego at the door. No one is perfect.

<u>Selling to a team</u>

Often we would be presenting to a group of the prospects team. For those who sell complex products, such as mainframe computers, specialized equipment and mass scale manufacturing, you already face that.

As I mentioned before about selling to bankers, they had the ubiquitous committee at their disposal as a strategy to put you off and then say no. I'm sure most corporations have the budget committee or the R&D guys to send you to see; and you never get back to the sales leader who can make the real decision.

Our solution to that was when they would say they needed to discuss our proposal with their accountant or lawyer or executive committee, we insisted, and I do mean we always insisted, that we do that for them. We told them it was our job, not theirs, to win the bank's approval.

If we let a banker try and present our program, we lost the sale nearly every time. The average banker could barely spell bank owned life insurance much less tell someone else what is was and how it funded a deferred compensation program. So we insisted.

When you are one team selling to another team, there should always be three to five parties sitting at that buyers table.

One prospect is the relationship manager, the one we originally opened the door with. Based on the size of the bank it was either the CEO or the CFO. In a corporation it is a buyer in the acquisition department who is most likely a non-expert.

Another prospect is the internal accountant or an investment officer (the end user). In non-bank sales this would be the end user of what you are selling whether a computer system, a cooling system, or a metal forming press.

A third prospect team member is the final decision maker, and in very large organizations this party is rarely at the early sales process meetings.

And sometimes a member of the budgeting committee is there; or lurking behind the scenes.

In every case, it is upon you, the sales team leader, to figure this out and assign the roles and responsibilities to your team members to move the process forward.

And don't forget, in complex sales progress is being invited back – sometimes over and over – but always moving closer to the decision to buy it from your team.

Conclusion

Sales. Perhaps the single most brutal profession there is. Not because it is physically brutal, like playing football or cage fighting, but because it is mentally and emotionally brutal.

And that is all because the single greatest enemy to a salesman's success is the person he sees in the mirror every day. Yes, the salesman's greatest obstacle to success is himself or herself.

"How can that be?" you ask.

You have just read that I was my own greatest obstacle to my success. I had (and still have) call reluctance. I don't know why as I have read book after book on calling prospects, and I can roleplay a great phone call over and over.

But when I reach for that phone, I would rather reach for a Cobra ready to strike.

Allow me to ask you a question. Would you rather be great at making phone calls; or great at closing sales?

As you have read I had to find workarounds, and I did so over and over and thus succeeded as a premier salesman – because I love to sell and can close almost anyone.

I truly love the mental challenge of winning over a person or a room full of directors to my way of thinking.

It has been said that the art of diplomacy is the ability to get the other person to have your way.

Remember that and you will succeed in sales.

Good luck.

ABOUT the AUTHOR

Lynn O. High is an experienced financial author and life insurance and securities salesman.

Lynn became a life insurance agent truly by accident as you will learn shortly in this book, and over the years was very successful in his unplanned sales career.

For anyone in sales, and in any industry, the challenges and obstacles that Mr. High turns into lessons learned during his selling career and featured in this book will result in any salesperson, whether new or with years of experience, in gaining a new insights into the sales process and lead one to greater levels of success.

He is quoted as saying, "I often bought a book on sales and if I could find one idea, one phrase, one way to overcome an obstacle from that book then the time spent reading it was worth thousands of dollars in sales for me."

It is never too late to learn to earn.

Mr. High holds a bachelor's degree in economics and a master's degree in business administration. He is a retired U.S. Air Force officer having served twenty years as a fighter pilot flying over 450 combat missions during two combat tours in the Vietnam War.

His original book, Pay Yourself First, has been revised and is available at the Createspace book store. To take a look go to createspace.com and once on the main screen go the drop down box about two-thirds to the right next to the search box. Click the dropdown arrow and select "store." Then just enter my name, Lynn High, in the search box and you can see all of my works.

www.ingramcontent.com/pod-product-compliance
Lightning Source LLC
Chambersburg PA
CBHW051700170526
45167CB00002B/474